SISTER
IN A
BROTHERHOOD

Praise for Sister in a Brotherhood

"In *Sister in a Brotherhood*, Cindie Schooner-Ball tells her story of nearly three decades working in what was widely perceived as a man's career path, firefighting. She brings the reality of her adventures (and a few misadventures, too) home to the reader in a fascinating, lively style. Whether you're a firefighter or not, you'll want to read this account of life in the firehouse by a woman who helped open its doors to other women."

—*Scott Orr, Producer/Host,* Code 3—The Firefighters' Podcast

"A tribute to the people she served and the people she served with, Cindie Schooner-Ball's *Sister in a Brotherhood* chronicles the highs and lows of her life as a female firefighter."

—*Mark B. Williams, Vice President (retired),*
Oregon Health & Science University

"Utilizing a gritty, realistic style, Cindie Schooner-Ball captures the career life cycle that few outside of the fire service can imagine. She deftly peels back the public perception and smacks the reader in the face with the brutal reality firefighters face in their daily lives, on and off the job."

— *Mike Uskoski, Retired Fire Captain,*
29 years in Portland Fire and Rescue

"If you're considering a career as a firefighter/EMT, or paramedic, this is the book for you. Reading it brought back so many memories of my time in the Fire Service, as I was also a *Sister in a Brotherhood*. As Cindie Schooner-Ball points out, the Fire Service is very rewarding, yet very demanding, and you take the good with the bad. She is spot on with advice, too! Pay attention, highlight the important parts, and take the lessons she has generously conveyed in the book for your time in the fire service!"

— *Captain Teri Roberts, Broward Sheriff's Office*

"*Sister in Brotherhood* grabs the emotion, challenges and episodes of a woman pursuing the exciting life as a firefighter and EMT. The insight of Cindie Schooner-Ball's personal life, training regimen, career progression and actual emergencies makes an easy read and a book you can't put down."

— David W. Dunbar, Chairman & CEO (retired),
Synovus Bank of Florida

"An honest and enjoyable read, *Sister in a Brotherhood* reveals the extra levels of self-belief and determination it sometimes takes to succeed, especially when you aren't like the others around you."

— Vinnie Greico, Broward Sheriff Fire-Rescue, Retired Captain

"Cindie Schooner-Ball has done an excellent job of providing a window into a unique perspective on growing up, finding a living, and excelling in the face of adversity. I recommend this to anyone coming of age, feeling like a fish out of water, or wondering if civil service is for you."

— Robert S. Lewis, Architect

"Captain Schooner-Ball has masterfully re-created her career in her book, *Sister in a Brotherhood*. Once you begin to read, it isn't easy to put the book down.

I remember meeting Cindie at the beginning of her career. She always had a great work ethic. I was fortunate to watch her advance through every career rank, including obtaining her paramedic certification. She put 100 percent effort into everything she did, and it showed.

I recommend this book not just for members of the fire service but for anyone seeking to improve their chances of succeeding in this thing we call life."

— Allan London, Lieutenant (retired), Broward Sheriff Fire-Rescue

SISTER IN A BROTHERHOOD

Stories *from* My Life *as a* Female Firefighter

CINDIE SCHOONER-BALL

For Mark

My special beacon of light

CONTENTS

PROLOGUE

END OF THE BEGINNING,
Part 1

I pulled a crumpled wad of Kleenex out of my jacket pocket and dabbed the sweat beads on my face ever so lightly, trying not to ruin my makeup. After all, this was my moment, my retirement ceremony, almost thirty years in the making. Prior to joining the fire service, I'd been a card-carrying member of the job-of-the-week club, with my longest gigs lasting perhaps a year at most. Back then, I never dreamed I'd find a career that would drive me for nearly three full decades. Twenty-eight years, to be exact, and I'd requested the ceremony be held on the anniversary of the day that I began my illustrious career: June 8, 1987. That in itself was a testament to my love of the fire service.

In all my years on duty, I only wore lip gloss and eyebrow mascara, so it seemed funny that I was primped and polished for an event that would last maybe an hour, closing the most epic chapter of my life. I looked in the mirror one last time, first scanning the reflection of the station bathroom behind me and noting yet again that it was in dire need of TLC, including a paint color other than pasty oatmeal and some modern pictures to replace the cheap flower prints in plastic purple frames. They were undoubtedly scavenged from some firefighter's house when they should have been thrown in the trash years ago. This bathroom had looked the same for the last twenty years, for Christ's sake, even though it was located in one of our nicer, newer stations. It was long overdue for an HGTV-style makeover.

But enough of that. I focused on my reflection and smiled back at the image in the mirror. I worked extremely hard at staying slim, strong, and confident. Oh, I'd indulged in delicious food and drink on my off days, and like everybody else, I'd tried every diet known to man to keep weight off. But I had an advantage in that I loved to exercise, and my body was muscular from years of working out. Running kept me sane, along with jumping rope. I liked to put on my headphones, tune out the world, and get into my own thoughts. As I studied my reflection, I felt proud that all my hard work had continued to pay off, and my dress uniform still fit perfectly. The dark blue polyester ensemble looked good, with the patent leather shoes and belt shining in the mirror, and the crisp white shirt under a fitted jacket displaying my gold captain's badge, my twenty-five-years-of-service pin (they came in increments of five years), and other various "Atta girl" pins I'd been awarded over the years. My thick blonde hair was French braided and heavily sprayed, tucked up and held in place with a large barrette so it would stay put underneath my dress hat—similar to the way I'd worn it to accommodate my helmet all those years on duty. With one last nod at my reflection, I turned around to exit the sterile, outdated bathroom one last time as a civil servant. What a ride this has been.

My ceremony was held at Fire Rescue Station 67, in Weston, Florida, where I had worked for the last six months of my career. I'd been offered the bid on a rescue truck, which meant a small pay increase, and the station housed an additional rescue and one engine. These last several months weren't my first time working in this station on the edge of the Everglades. I had floated into this station many times before as a tailboard firefighter, an upgrade driver-engineer, a lieutenant, and finally as a captain. There were three other stations that covered the west side of Broward County, including two others in Weston and a newer one in the Everglades. I had worked at all of them. They were somewhat modern, with three large bays each, and gym equipment, including ellipticals, stationary bikes, treadmills, and good, old-fashioned free weights. It wasn't fancy, but it was effective, and working out with my crew remains a fond memory for me. We'd get dinner started and then blast music in the bay while we worked to stay physically and mentally fit. We wore our assorted workout clothes, of course, but if a call came in during gym time, we'd grab our pants, kick off our sneakers, get dressed, and respond quickly. We might continue our workouts after we came back from the call, but sometimes we'd just want showers, jumpsuits, and food. After dinner, we'd put the coffee on, maybe fix a dessert, and then sit outside together on lawn chairs, chatting about calls, family, and how much time we all had until retirement. Sometimes a chief would join us, but either way, this time was priceless. I felt lucky to be a part of this special family.

The captain that I was replacing at Station 67 had retired early, fighting cancer, and she was both my mentor and friend. I had spoken to her many times about the station dynamics, and although I knew I could never replace her, I'd vowed to do my best to run the station efficiently. She was a brilliant paramedic, and I had run many calls with her over the years. But the one that really cemented our friendship and my respect for her was one she wasn't even on. I was a fire lieutenant on an engine at the time, and she and her partner had just stopped in to say hello when the call came in to respond to a gas leak. We'd just finished up dinner, and we left the station with all of the plates still on the table, and the kitchen was a mess. The call lasted for hours, and we were exhausted. But we weren't done yet. We'd have to get all our equipment cleaned and put back in service before we could even think about cleaning up the kitchen. So, imagine our surprise when we returned to the station and the dinner table was cleared off, the dishes clean, and the kitchen spotless. I couldn't believe it. Nobody ever did this kind of thing. Yet, she had taken her time while on duty, and instead of resting at her station, she and her partner decided to help us out. It was a welcome gift, and when I tried to thank her, she just smiled and said it was the right thing to do. I never forgot that act of kindness.

The bay looked different today, all "dressed up" for the ceremony, than it had on all those afternoons and evenings I recalled so fondly. All the trucks and workout equipment had been moved out to make space for the ceremony, and the beautiful red fire trucks had been lined up and parked outside of the bay window, washed and waxed for this special occasion. Both on- and off-duty personnel and friends and family were gathering to see the pomp and circumstance, and the honor guard regiment was lined up outside. They looked resplendent as they stood ramrod straight in their dress uniforms next to the Black Pearl Pipes and Drums Band, waiting to escort me inside. I was soaking it up, taking in every moment and creating permanent mental photographs I could reflect on in the future to recall the beautiful ceremony about to take place in my honor.

There was a podium set up for speeches and a table next to it displayed old photographs of me, along with a triangular wooden case holding a United States flag that had flown over my station for three days. My name, rank, and dates of hire and retirement were etched into the case. It was beautiful, but my most prized possession sat next to it: my cherished helmet, which had protected me for many years, looking suitably worn. The display was rounded out with a new gold captain's badge that had been placed inside of a wallet next to my new picture ID, which said "retired."

My various badges were also lined up side by side, starting with my beloved first badge, engraved with the number ninety-nine. I was hired along with ten other people, and even still, the department was supposed to fail. The many cities in Broward County had wanted their own individual departments, though they didn't have the means to fund them, and they were fighting viciously against operating a singular department for the whole county. The outlook was grim, so the Broward County fire chief handed us our precious first badges without any fanfare. "Congratulations," he said, "but I don't know how long you guys will have this job."

None of us cared. Although we were not fully ignorant of the bad blood or city politics, we were too young, hungry, and motivated to care. It turns out the chief—and the rest of the higher-ups— had underestimated the tenacity of the little redheaded stepchild department of which I was now a proud member.

We fought tooth and nail to keep it going and would continue the fight until the county sheriff, Ken Jenne, brought both fire and EMS under his jurisdiction, and a few of the other smaller departments opted to merge with us to save themselves. We became the first fire department in the country to merge with law enforcement and other county departments, and once that was complete, we were an incredibly powerful fire-rescue organization. But what a way to start!

I would always cherish that very first badge as a symbol of all the hardship I had overcome to get where I was and of the struggles our department overcame to even remain in service. And the fact that I was starting out my career wearing number 99, just like the fierce female secret agent in the 1960s TV show *Get Smart*, seemed particularly auspicious. Agent 99 was a pioneer in her own right, and to share her number felt like destiny.

Where have all the years gone? I thought while waiting for my ceremony to begin. That green firefighter, a trailblazer just like Agent 99, once so optimistic and fearless, was now much older and wiser, having experienced both the very best and the very worst of human nature. And now I was looking at freedom. It remained to be seen how I would navigate my unknown but well-earned future. All I knew on the day of my retirement ceremony was that, if asked to do it all over again, I would without hesitation.

As I looked at those badges, so many memories—good, bad, funny, and tragic—came flooding back, and I felt the ghosts of the past, of people who lived and others who died regardless of how hard my crew and I tried to save them. I tried not to focus on the table—or the memories it inspired—too much, because it wasn't time for tears yet. Instead, I looked up, swallowing the lump in my throat. "Mom, Dad, and big brother, I hope you're proud of who I've become," I whispered softly, listening as the morning breeze carried my words to their heavenly ears until the band's off-key practice run jolted me back to the present.

"Captain, we will begin the ceremony in just a few minutes," said the chief. "Are you ready?"

"Yes, Chief, I am." The tall man in front of me, a former Marine, was resplendent in bugles and ribbons. I had requested that he accompany me at the ceremony. He had been on the job almost as long as myself, and I had fond memories of working calls, both good and bad, with him long before he became a chief. We shared some history, and he had always been a class act.

"Attention!" The honor guard's call was the cue. No turning back now.

All uniformed personnel lined up, and as the ceremony began, a flurry of emotions threatened my calm demeanor. I looked out into the bay at the rows of men and women looking polished and professional in their Class A uniforms. Some were already sweating profusely in the still, humid morning air, and I couldn't blame them. There is nothing quite like polyester in the hot Florida climate. I only hoped and prayed that nobody dropped from heat exhaustion, though if they did, they were in the right place.

I grabbed the arm of the chief, who was ready to escort me into the bay, accompanied by the Black Pearl Pipes and Drums band and the Honor Guard, and lead me directly up to the podium to stand beside him. He smiled at me and whispered, "You've earned this. Enjoy the moment."

The first order of the ceremony was for me to inspect my crew one last time. I walked over to them, smiling, then hugged some and shook hands with others, thanking all of them for wishing me well. It was a poignant moment as I thought back to the time I'd spent running calls with them, trying not to be too much of a ballbuster.

When I was their captain, I felt guilty about not eating with them all the time, which had been mandatory when I got hired. "You eat with the family" was the creed of most firehouses back then, and it should still be that way for the most part. But in the age of paperwork, station problems, internet training, community events, and running calls, that rule got harder and harder to follow. And being the captain of the station required some separation from the crew, too. They needed to be able to let their hair down among themselves, and frankly, I needed some space in my own private bunkroom/office to get things done before the eight o'clock shift change each morning. Still, I had truly enjoyed the time I spent with them and had great respect for every member of my crew.

Firefighters are a different breed. Most of us are proud, loyal men and women who have thick skins and lion hearts. We're fierce, calm, and willing to do what is necessary, putting our own comforts last for the good of the citizens we serve. We show up on your worst day, during your biggest crisis, and we do our best to create a positive outcome.

You must be tough to do this work. Hell, our dinner conversations would make many people run for the hills, but there is something to be said for a crew who can take a bite out of their juicy sandwiches while discussing the bloody scene of a suicide, car wreck, domestic violence call, or any other tragedy we'd just returned from—or who can ask somebody to pass the potatoes or meat between descriptions of brains, body parts, and all manner of bodily fluids. On occasion, we'd review photos we'd taken during a call over dinner, asking what was done or not and critiquing our performance among ourselves. It was our personal way to vent to each other in the private confines of our family table, releasing our emotions in an effort to prevent those images from imprinting permanently on our memories and souls.

Don't let our tough exteriors fool you—we most certainly cry, suffer, and deal with ghosts that never leave our memory banks. We all deal with it differently: Some pick up excessive bad habits while others leave the profession altogether. As for me, well, I made room for those images in the library of my memories.

I learned a long time ago that you cannot save everyone, even if you're a firefighter. We are not God or whatever higher power you do or do not believe in. But, as long as we give everything we have to save those we can, we can learn to accept that we cannot control the order of life.

My EMT instructor gave the class three rules on our very first day:

1. You must have empathy, not sympathy.

2. Their crisis is not your crisis.

3. Stress is what you create for yourself.

I try to live by those rules every day, and I've added one more that I learned in fire academy: Be aware, because if the rescuer goes down, who will rescue the rescuer?

"Inspection complete," I told the chief, walking back to meet him behind the podium. The speeches and accolades that followed were, to be honest, a mixed bag. Some were genuine and truly touching while others were generic speeches from people, including the mayor, whom I didn't know personally. But that was okay. As they spoke, I looked into the crowd, smiling as I recognized and acknowledged the people who really had made a positive impact on my career, had my back, and helped me overcome my insecurities.

These people had also told me the unvarnished truth, reading me the riot act when I screwed up and deserved to hear it. Looking out into the crowd, I swear I could see their faces in the shadows in the background of the bay. Some of the people I had run calls on with various crews all over the area were staring back at me, and I knew they would remain with me for life.

As I surveyed my friends and colleagues, I couldn't help but notice how great the retired guys looked. They wore shorts, Hawaiian shirts, and deck shoes or flip-flops. Some sported gray beards and long hair that flew in the face of the strict grooming requirements they'd had to follow throughout their careers. Most of them looked at least ten years younger now that they were no longer stressing about calls, enduring sleepless nights, training in the hellacious Florida summers, or putting up with the idiots who managed to climb the career ladder faster than they ever did despite an utter lack of common sense. (There are two sayings among the old-timers: "Common sense isn't common anymore," and "Your people can make you or break you." I never forgot those crucial pieces of advice.)

I had been a bit envious of those carefree retirees for a while, but when the time came for me to step up to the podium to say a few words, the finality of this day, this moment—the end of the structured life I'd known for the past twenty-eight years—started to sink in, and it hit me hard. *No crying in the firehouse!* As I pulled my five-by-seven notecards out of my dress jacket pocket, took a breath, and looked out into the crowd of civilians seated in the far corner, I saw my husband, my special beacon of light, smiling proudly back at me. A calmness suddenly took over my emotions, and I knew everything was going to be all right.

ONE

HIDDEN PAST REARS ITS GOLDEN FEATHER

The small, insignificant sign posted in the lower corner of the message board in the unemployment office caught my eye. In all the years I'd been in between crappy jobs, I had never thought about signing up for unemployment, much less setting foot inside the actual office to file. I had been raised to get a job, not a handout, and I'd always managed to find another restaurant to waitress in, or an office job to pay the bills, but my luck had run out, and this time I was desperate. I'd been on my own since the age of sixteen, and my parents didn't have any money to lend me. My mother was basically destitute herself; my brother lived with her to help out. My dad was just cold. I knew he wouldn't give me a dime, and it would crush me to even ask him. He made money as a stone mason, but he spent whatever he had on himself or his lady friends. So, I was already on edge when I walked through the door, and to see that sign and realize the most unlikely part of my past might just be my golden ticket was a shock, to say the least.

The sign read, "If you are an American Indian, call this number." Was this a sign from above, or was it foolishness to cash in on my heritage at this point in my life? It had caused me so much humiliation growing up that I had learned to be ashamed of it.

My great-grandfather on my father's side was a full-blooded Mohawk Indian, and though I never knew him, his legacy haunted my childhood. In the small Ohio town where I grew up, being of Indian heritage was not anything to be proud of. This was the land of cornfields, blue eyes, and blond hair, and dark skin was not welcomed. I never had any Black friends, because there weren't any Black people around to get acquainted with, except one kid whose father was a dentist in town. Besides, my father would never have let me associate with people of color. He was the most racist man I have ever known, which is pretty ironic since he looked like a classic Indian brave. He was very handsome, standing over six feet tall with dark, red-brown skin and a straight nose. Unfortunately, however, he passed some of those looks down to my brother and me, which led to endless taunting by the mean kids in school. They called me "Pocahontas," and they called my six-foot-eight brother "Squawman" until the day he died of cancer at the young age of fifty-seven.

I remember walking down the church aisle in my long choir robe on Sundays. I could hear the hypocrites whispering and feel them judging me. They knew of my parents, who never stepped foot into the church, probably because of the same treatment I got there. They knew I had a hell-raising alcoholic father (who'd gotten mean when he got sober) and a sweet but pitiful mother who continued to love him regardless of his womanizing. My mother's father was a Baptist minister who rode horseback preaching in the hollers of Kentucky, and my father's sister was a Pentecostal preacher and faith healer who baptized me and then subsequently scared me to death whenever I had to go to her church and watch her "heal" people. So, my parents had both been exposed to religion from an early age and turned away from it. My mother always said, "God gave you a brain to think, so use it," and religion didn't align with that principle.

Needless to say, my childhood was a struggle for many reasons, but the way I saw it, my great-grandfather, the Mohawk Indian who'd been born on the banks of the Sandusky River in Northwest Ohio and lost his parents during the cholera epidemic in the 1800s, was the root of all my trouble. But now, he just might be my salvation.

I had a simple note, notarized by a judge and confirming my Native American heritage, tucked away in a drawer somewhere. My great-grandfather had signed the letter with a large "X" because he wasn't able to read or write. My mother had given it to me many years before, but I'd never thought much of it, and I had certainly never

TO WHOM IT MAY CONCERN:-

I, Thomas Franklin Schooner Sr., do hereby solemnly swear that this statement is true in all respects to the best of my knowledge.

I am a full blooded American Mohawk Indian, having been told the same by my father, who died when I was a boy.

My Mother, I do not remember, as she died during the cholera epidemic during the early eighteen hundreds.

I was born, so I am told, between Fremont and Sandusky, Ohio, on the Sandusky river in the State of Ohio.

Thomas Franklin his X Schooner
mark

Sworn to and subscribed before me this 22nd day of March, A.D. 1935.

Lolita Prentice

Lolita Prentice, Notary Public.
My Commission expires July 7, 1936.
Wood County, Ohio.

imagined that it would turn out to be the golden ticket to my future.

So, how did I get there, reading that note in the Fort Lauderdale unemployment office? Let's rewind twelve years, to 1974. I had left home and moved in with my boyfriend and his two male roommates shortly after we started dating. The roommates were both solid, good-hearted guys. I was seventeen, and they were a few years older than me, but they welcomed me into their fold, looking out for me like a little sister. At the time we all moved in together, I hadn't graduated from high school because I lacked one and a half credits—in PE, of all things. I was too busy hitchhiking to Cocoa Beach and having fun in the sun with my friends to care much, but I would pay the price ten years later—in 1984, to be exact, when I went back to high school in Fort Lauderdale to complete the new requirements. It was a big pain in the ass, but I didn't want to live my life saying, "Do you want fries with that?"

Anyway, in the summer of 1974, the four of us and two dogs, a white German shepherd named Sage and a bluetick hound named (what else?) Blue, moved to Tampa. At first, we rented a room in an old hotel. We had two queen beds, and the guys slept in one while my boyfriend and I slept in the other. These new digs were about as bad as growing up in poverty, but this time, there was no safety net. Either I got a job fast or we'd run out of money and become homeless. So, I got a job fast. I started working as a teller in downtown Tampa at a Spanish bank called Banco Popular. This was a no-brainer for me since I had worked in other banks while in the DACA program in high school and another bank in Cocoa Beach. I didn't remember a word of Spanish from high school, but I decided to just wing it. Besides, I got to wear a variety of seventies-chic navy polyester uniform suits with red, white, and blue blouses and the requisite rayon bow tied at the neck. Hey, they came free with the job, and

I didn't make enough money to afford an alternative wardrobe. Cut-off shorts, T-shirts, and flip-flops were my preferred clothing.

Fortunately, the hotel stay was short. The guys worked as landscapers, and their bosses let us move into a dumpy house next to the office, where rent was free. Our power was always getting shut off, but we would run extension cords to the office to keep our lights on.

Free lodging aside, and despite all of us having jobs, we were just about broke. Most of the week, we all lived on peanut butter and jelly on white bread, but sometimes on a Friday night, I would hit the supermarket in a big ass, deep-pocketed coat from the Goodwill store, and I would swipe a couple of steaks and some beer. I'm not proud of that, but Jimmy Buffett's "Peanut Butter Conspiracy" song about stealing from the mini-mart rang true for a lot of poor folks in the seventies. We were so hungry for a real meal, and we never meant any harm. Those steaks were the highlight of the month when we could get them. On one occasion, Blue decided to grab one for himself off the grill, and he devoured it before we could even react. I really thought his master was going to beat him to death. That dog was lucky we loved him that night.

Tampa was harsh in those days, and the streets were mean if you were poor. Of course, there were parts of the area that were beautiful, like the beach, but those areas were far from my reality. I had to hitchhike to work because our car had gotten repossessed, again, and I had a frightening experience one morning. The guy who picked me up kept driving away from where I needed to be and eventually, he pulled off the road in the grass and stopped the car. I could see the tall buildings of downtown in the distance, but we were in a fairly desolate area. I remembered to always check the car door when getting in to make sure it was kept unlocked with my hand on it just in case. This was the "just in case" moment. I immediately opened the door, jumped out, and started running. "Hey, young lady," he yelled at me. "I really thought you were a working girl!" I thought, *Oh, yeah, sure, eighteen-year-old me in this rayon-and-polyester getup: a striped blouse with a giant bow, jacket, and polyester blue pants.*

"No," I yelled back at him, crying, "I am just trying to get to work." I swear angels exist, and there was certainly one with me that day. When he pulled up next to me in his car and asked if I was all right, I climbed into the front seat and shut the door. He dropped me off in front of the Banco Popular. That was definitely a lesson from heaven above, and I never hitchhiked by myself again. In fact, my very last time hitchhiking at all was that same year. I was with my boyfriend, and we were both sitting in this guy's front seat, me in the middle. When we got to our destination, my boyfriend slid out of the car, but the guy grabbed me and held on until my boyfriend yanked me out of his grip and out of the car. That was enough of a warning for me. I never hitchhiked again.

One of the guys who lived with us loved to party. He played guitar, sang beautifully, and looked like a rock star. Big blue eyes, long blond hair, and a million-dollar smile. He loved the girls, and they loved him back. His family was wealthy, and they lived up north, but he'd left it all for Florida. He'd been dating a nurse, and he married her while we were all living in Tampa, but he never stopped partying. As fate would have it, he was driving home drunk one night, got into a head-on collision, and was killed instantly.

We were devastated by the loss, and not too long after, the three of us moved back to Cocoa Beach for a short period of time before we decided to move south to Fort Lauderdale in 1977. I got another job as a bank teller, working with two other girls in a walkup window in what was, back then, the tallest building in downtown

Fort Lauderdale. I rode my bicycle to work, skirt and all. I fractured my coccyx when I hit a pothole one rainy morning, but it was still safer than hitchhiking.

Fast-forward eight years, to 1985. I was still living in Fort Lauderdale with the same boyfriend (no roommates at this point). I'd finally finished high school, and I'd gone to cosmetology school, all fifteen hundred hours of it. My "career" had been a series of jobs like the ones I just described, mixed in with as much modeling work as I could get. My boyfriend had become a firefighter, and I went to visit him for dinner occasionally, but this conversation came up at the firehouse one night.

"I think you should go to the fire academy and become a firefighter," said the chief, who was sitting next to me at the dinner table. "It's an up-and-coming field for women, and you're in fantastic shape. You have a good personality and an even temperament. Plus, you'd fit in great with the guys."

The guys on shift stopped eating and stared at me expectantly. I, on the other hand, looked at the chief like he was completely out of his mind. He must surely have a hole in his head. He must be missing his brain. I had dabbled in many vocations, including secretary/model, waitress/model, and bank teller/wannabee model. Lately, I'd been considering using my hard-earned cosmetology certificate to do hair, nails, and skincare in the hopes of becoming a professional makeup artist in addition to modeling. I couldn't think of anything that would qualify me *less* than firefighting. I had helped my boyfriend pay for fire academy, but the most involved I intended to be with the firehouse was to look pretty when I visited him there. Now here was the chief, telling me I might as well be one of the guys?

"You're kidding me, right?" I said, looking down the long table at the guys on shift, waiting for them to start laughing at the joke.

But they didn't. One after another spoke up, agreeing with the chief.

"You run and work out all the time," they said, "and you're in better shape than most of the guys here, so why not?" They told me they'd help me get through fire school and offered to let me train with them, rolling hoses, carrying ladders, and learning about the equipment to get a head start in the academy.

"No, I don't think so," I said, "but thanks anyway for the support."

A few months later, the wheels of fate intervened, and my life suddenly took a spin in a completely different direction. My boyfriend—my first love—and I were bored to tears, at least I was, but still very dependent upon each other, frustrated because of differences in expectations perceived for our continued future together. I loved him, but I was no longer in love with him. He was six-and-a-half years older than me and certainly more streetwise, and I was both financially dependent on him and scared to venture out on my own. But still, I had grown up, and I desired so much more out of life at that point. I don't know if I would have left him as quickly as he left me, but in hindsight, I am happy he did. It pushed me to grow up and think about how I wanted to live my life on my own terms.

One morning—Valentine's Day, 1985, to be exact—he decided he'd had enough. He announced that he no longer loved me, then he called my older sister in Texas (who had raised me since the age of thirteen), and said, "Come get her."

Despite my unhappiness with him, being dumped like that felt abrupt and cold after twelve years of living together. I was in shock, as though the rug had been suddenly pulled out from under my feet. I had no way of knowing then how great my life would turn out, absent of a crystal ball, and I spent many tearful nights and black days of depression in Texas, running to keep myself sane. I lost thirty pounds that I really couldn't afford to lose, finally developing the ultra-skinny model physique required by the agencies I had signed with when I was younger.

I was in a whirlwind of uncertainty. I was grateful for the love of my sister, brother-in-law, and nephew (who I swear was a wise old soul in a thirteen-year-old body). But after three months of living in a state that, frankly, I hated, I missed my beloved Florida. I spent those three months working in downtown Houston at the Burger King headquarters, and as soon as I'd saved enough money, I flew home, landing in a black thunderstorm that felt incredibly fitting.

Back in Fort Lauderdale, I rented a tiny studio by the month, just down the street from the apartment where I had lived with my boyfriend. I was still so lovesick that I would watch out the window, waiting for him to drive by while I cried my eyes out. I felt so alone, but in hindsight, I think a lot of people can relate to feeling this kind of desperation when you're alone.

The good news, though, was that I got to reunite with my beloved cat, Bogey. He was an orange-and-white tabby with green eyes. He looked just like Garfield, and I loved him so much. My dad would never allow me to have a cat because he thought they were filthy. He'd brought home a curly tailed fox as a pet once, and we had a goose named Matilda until she mysteriously disappeared around Thanksgiving one year. We'd had a couple of dogs growing up, too, but never a feline. I had always wanted one, though, so Bogey was beloved. My best friend, who lived in the same building as my boyfriend, told me that Bogey wanted nothing to do with my boyfriend and his new girlfriend. He was as thrilled with our reunion as I was.

With Bogey at my side, I learned to stop crying over my ex and pushed forward. I applied for a secretarial position with an international insurance company downtown, and wouldn't you know, I got the job! If nothing else, this would restore my confidence and pay my bills. The swanky office was an improvement from my banking jobs, where I'd sat in bare-bones walkup windows counting other people's money.

This large company self-insured all of the thoroughbred and harness horse racetracks in the world, in addition to the many dog tracks. I was hired to be the president's right-hand girl, and although I wasn't a professional secretary by any means, I took dictation, answered phone calls, made appointments, and learned to handle anything required for this enviable position.

The 1980s were still a unique time for working women. Word was that you were better off seeking out male bosses because female bosses who'd made it into management positions were mean and calculating, especially toward female underlings. Who could really blame them? They had to be tough as nails to hang onto their positions, because niceness was misinterpreted as weakness.

So, I'd found a male boss, and he was fantastic. But most of my co-workers hated me because I had landed such a coveted position without much experience. It didn't help that I'd caught the eye of the president's son, which inspired jealousy and backstabbing from the other girls in the office. He was very handsome—the target of all of the single girls in the office. He took me to dinner at his favorite sushi restaurant, and although I absolutely hate sushi, I managed to choke it down. Cuisine choice aside, I knew there was no future with this guy. He was handsome and sweet, but there was zero chemistry between us.

Still, I was very fond of the president and respected him enormously. He was an alumnus of Notre Dame, with famous friends like the Shula's and other community icons. I loved dressing up for work in my favorite pencil skirt, blouse, makeup, and heels. (There wasn't a trace of polyester anywhere in my wardrobe.) And I thought it was exciting to go get him lunch from all of the hot spots downtown. He never talked down to me or ever said anything inappropriate. He gave me a chance, and he was always kind—even when I showed up for my first day with my head shaved.

When I got hired at the insurance company, I had beautiful, thick, shoulder-length auburn hair that I curled with an iron every day. I liked the curls, but I didn't like to spend time curling it, so having recently finished cosmetology school, I decided to give myself a perm on the Saturday before I officially started my new job. Bad choice. I had recently chemically lightened my hair, and the perm solution didn't agree with the other chemicals, so my hair melted and came out looking like a Brillo pad.

Long story short, I came to work the following Monday with a shaved head. I looked like a "tween" boy, and I dreaded the reactions I'd get in the office. My boss, the president, just stared at me with a bemused look on his face. "Are you the same girl I hired last week?" he asked, but that was the only comment he ever made about it. He treated the office staff very well, and he threw fancy, catered holiday parties.

Despite all the pros of the job, however, I lacked the basic mentality or passion needed to thrive in my role. I was expected to be the first person there in the morning and the last person to leave at night. And according to the vice president's right-hand girl, I had to willingly show up to work on the weekends, too. Are you kidding me? I had absolutely no intention of giving up my weekends, especially for free, just to show how dedicated I was to the company. So, as life would have it, the wheels began to turn, and I was fired one week shy of my one-year anniversary, which would have given me a one-week paid vacation.

Damn it!

Now what?

I was running out of funds quickly. The studio was paid up for the month, but that was coming up fast. I was proud, had never collected unemployment, could always get a waitress job. Damn.

In the modeling world, although I was twenty-eight, I could still pass for a teenager or an eighteen-year-old. But I had enough life experience—and maybe even a little wisdom—to realize that the idea of pretending to be a kid for a potential modeling job just had a bad ring to it. Besides, modeling was a cutthroat business, and unless you lived in NYC or Miami, it was a constant hustle just to survive. Once, when I was younger and seriously pursuing that elusive career path, I had won the title of "Miss Car Cents" in an annual West Palm Beach beauty contest judged by automobile aficionados. It didn't make me famous or rich, but it did earn me the prize of a week on a Windjammer cruise. My boyfriend did not approve of me taking a vacation like that by myself, though, so I never went.

Anyway, I was nearing my expiration date in the modeling world, and although I had always been able to get a waitressing job, I knew I needed to find something more stable this time and with better pay.

Desperation was beginning to set in, and moving back to Texas with my sister was not an option, so it was off to the unemployment office, which brings us back to where we started.

I was at a crossroads in my life. I just couldn't stomach the thought of working thirty years in a bank—or any office—or worse yet, as a career waitress. I'd had a few opportunities to acquire a sugar daddy, but that thought made my skin crawl. I just wanted to sink my teeth into a career that meant something. To truly make a difference and try to help others. As I stared at that sign—"If you are an American Indian, call this number."—I suddenly remembered the conversation I'd had with the chief and the guys at the firehouse more than a year before, and it hit me. Maybe they were right!

What did I have to lose? I called the number on the sign and made an appointment to meet with a career specialist who worked for the Seminole Indian Tribe. She was very special, though not of Indian heritage herself. I showed her the letter from my great-grandfather and told her I dreamed of going to the fire academy but could not afford the $100 enrollment fee or the living expenses to make it through the process. Though my heritage was Mohawk and not Seminole, I was welcomed with open arms, and the organization provided me with the money to cover both my enrollment and living expenses. I was truly in shock.

What a miracle!

The one thing about myself that had always made me feel ashamed and embarrassed was going to elevate me into a wonderful career. My life was about to change in ways that I could never have imagined in a million years.

TWO

LET THE GAMES BEGIN

I passed the physical agility test and was officially enrolled in the fire academy in 1986. Although I had been exposed to the life of a firefighter through my ex-boyfriend, I was now going to experience this career, which had never been on my radar as a personal possibility, firsthand. I would be tested, both physically and mentally, more than would ever be possible in a "traditionally female" occupation.

Before I dive in, I want to make it clear that nothing I write in this book is intended to bash male firefighters or to scare readers away from the profession. Rather, I want to share with other women the honest truth of what I observed and experienced during my long journey, both in the fire academy before I was hired and throughout my career. Firefighting is an inherently dangerous profession, and there are a lot of tough aspects to it (the least of which is having to deal with the quirks and challenges of living in the firehouse for twenty-four hours at a time or more with many different—mostly male—personalities). If you think otherwise, I advise you to find another career.

As a new enrollee in the fire academy, I was scared, sure, but dammit, I was excited, too. I couldn't wait to push myself beyond what I thought I could endure. I was under no illusions about the danger of the job, and I knew I would have to train twice as hard to keep up with the men while learning to ignore any inappropriate comments they might throw my way. But I also knew I was no cupcake. I had the will of a lion, and I was determined to see just what I was truly made of.

I didn't fit the profile of what people thought a female firefighter should look like. I looked like a model, because that had been my dream. I loved fashion and had devoured magazines like *Seventeen*, *Glamour*, and *Vogue* since I was a kid. This was the complete opposite of what I was expected to look like in this career, and yet I never tried to change my appearance or worried that my looks would be a barrier to success. I just kept my nose to the grindstone, preparing myself for what was to come. Fire academy was all-consuming: five days a week, eight hours a day. I was thankful I didn't have a boyfriend or family obligations to worry about so I could focus entirely on myself. My only job was to give it everything I had and more, gaining confidence and becoming fearless. This skinny, dark-skinned young woman was going to be a firefighter!

Though I hadn't dreamed of becoming a firefighter until recently, I quickly realized this career had always been a perfect fit. My first memory of firefighters was from when I was six years old and my brother was twelve-and-a-half. My parents couldn't afford to buy us Christmas presents that year, so the firefighters brought gifts to our house. I got my first doll, a Chatty Cathy, and my brother got a bowling set. We were thrilled. Throughout my career, I would reflect on that time in my childhood as my crew and I handed out candy to the kids on Halloween, delivered Thanksgiving turkeys with all the fixings to families who otherwise wouldn't have a holiday meal, and especially as we delivered Christmas presents to area kids whose families couldn't afford them. It was truly a heartwarming experience for me and all of us, and it never ceased to amaze me that I had come full circle.

But helping others around the holidays like that is the easy part—anyone can do that if they just open their hearts. The rest of the job is a different story. So, what does it take to become a firefighter? Stability, steadiness, tenacity, persistence, stamina, and backbone. These qualities are necessary from fire academy all the way to retirement. This was true when I enrolled in the 1980s, and it's still true today.

Over the years, lots of people have asked me how long the actual process of getting hired takes. It's different for everyone, but in general, it can be a long production. It's not like most other jobs, where you fill out an application, get called in for an interview, and receive an offer letter in a couple of weeks.

Enrolling in the fire academy to get state certified is just the first step, and it can take a long time just to get your starting date. This is where perseverance, determination, and plain old grit come into play. If you're looking to take the first step into firefighting, I suggest you prepare physically, mentally, and logistically ahead of time. (For example, the easiest step that many people overlook is having all of the required documentation completed prior to enrolling.) Many people are under the impression that you sign up first, and then start preparing.

Negative, Ghost Rider. If you wait till you've started, it's too late.

When I finally registered for the fire academy, I met two police officers who worked for the municipality where I lived. The department wanted them to become fire certified as part of a new program for public safety officers. The idea was for the city to save money by having police officers be dual certified as firefighters. It was supposed to be more bang for the buck, according to the powers that be, but firefighters and cops are totally different breeds—for one, police officers are by definition looking to prevent crime, so many patients were unwilling to fess up to them with potentially life-saving information for fear of incriminating themselves—and the program ended up failing miserably.

Firefighters show up and save lives. They don't care about what drugs the patient has ingested, except that they need to know so they can be treated correctly. It seemed like an oxymoron to see them with medical gloves on and stethoscopes around their necks while visibly sporting a set of handcuffs secured on their belts. It made sense to merge firefighters and paramedics, but not law enforcement.

Regardless, these two guys and I became good friends, and they offered to drive me to school most mornings in the back of the police car. I rode behind the plexiglass barricade, and they would tease me the whole time about whether they would choose to let me out or not. They were good guys, and it was all in good fun. Besides, I was able to tease them right back. For example, one of the guys was scared of heights. He was a big, tough mammoth of a man—so big that he had to special order his bunker coat—and yet he froze whenever he had to climb a ladder. That was plenty of ammo for me, right there. Still, I tried not to bust his chops too much, because my beat-up Volkswagen was on its last legs, and my police friends were my most reliable ride.

The class consisted of both classroom and physical work. We started the day with running, which was by far the easiest part of the physical training because I'd already been doing it for years. But everything else was much more difficult. I distinctly remember struggling to use a rope to hoist a fifty-pound roll of two-and-a-half-inch hose up to the top of a twenty-four-foot ladder.

"Put some ass into it!" the instructor yelled at me. "Come on already! Use your legs! Those are the strongest muscles on a woman!" I didn't dare talk back to him. He was beyond intimidating, with his piercing blue eyes and his well-worn Boston Fire helmet cocked to one side. He was a seasoned firefighter with a northeastern attitude that meant he didn't sugarcoat anything. But he was fair, and he liked me because I showed him my determination, didn't mind sweating like a pig, and never played "the woman card." He was an icon with quite a reputation for being a top-notch firefighter and instructor, and his belief in me, combined with his ability to push me to do better, was a big part of my early success. Sadly, before I could thank him personally for all he did for me, I found out he'd died of cancer shortly after retirement.

The classroom portion of our work involved absorbing an enormous amount of information—and passing tests on all of it—as we built knowledge and confidence at every stage of our education. We learned basic fire behavior, the different kinds of extinguishers, and signs of flashovers and backdrafts. We learned when to fight fires offensively versus defensively and what different hydrant colors meant and how many gallons of water per minute they produced. We had timed evolutions, or drills, on everything from donning our bunker gear to raising and hoisting ladders to tying knots, securing areas, and dragging dummies out of burning buildings. We also learned basic medical skills such as bandaging, taking blood pressures and pulses, and recognizing signs of shock. And at the end of this training, we prepared for the final tests. A State of Florida fire instructor from Ocala, where the state fire college is located, came to our facility to administer the timed tests, and wouldn't you know it, *I passed!*

But my fire certification was just the start of my training.

When I began my career, firefighting was separate from emergency medicine with one exception: First responders needed basic medical skills, and they were all the more valuable if they were also emergency medical technicians, or EMTs for short. I decided I would sign up for that training immediately after getting my State of Florida fire certificate. It would also look good on my application when applying to test with different fire departments for potential hiring.

Today, the profession has evolved tremendously. If you decide to embark on this journey, firefighting and emergency medical technician certifications, along with an associate's degree in fire science, are all included in your training at the fire academy. The next step is to sign up for paramedic school, which is now a requirement for most progressive fire-rescue departments and a must to move up the promotional career ladder once you are hired. Believe me, becoming a paramedic is not for sissies either, but more on that later.

When I was starting my career, though, fire and EMT certifications were enough, so, armed with one and preparing for the other, I set out on a year-long effort to find myself a job.

During this time, I periodically checked in with the lady from the Seminole Indian Tribe, and she was so supportive. She told me I would be a great role model for young Native American girls, and I told her I would be honored to speak to them once I got hired.

The hiring process was tedious, to say the least. First, I had to research all the different fire departments in the areas to see who was even hiring. There was a message board in the fire academy office that listed the available or upcoming openings at the many departments in the state, each of which required candidates to pass yet another test before they could even be considered. I generally had to call human resources to get my name on the list for testing, but sometimes it was easier to drive to the downtown office to fill out the necessary paperwork.

Then there was the testing itself, which was required to get on the next list: the "to hire" list. The procedure for most fire departments consisted of a physical agility test and timed evolutions in which we dragged dummies, pulled hoses, climbed stairs, did pullups, ran laps, raised ladders, and completed other physical exercises. Then there was a written exam, and depending on your score, you were placed on a list of potential hires. The process was damn hard. And even passing the test wasn't a guarantee you'd land a job. Some of the tests were highly competitive, with dozens or more applicants for just a few spots. For example, five hundred or more people would show up for the Palm Beach County tests for a shot at being one of the two people they would ultimately hire. Fortunately, though, the "to hire" lists were good for several months—so if you didn't get the job right away, you didn't necessarily have to retake the test to be considered for the next opening.

I focused my efforts in Broward and Palm Beach counties, both because they were close to home and because the pay and benefits in those departments were better than elsewhere in the area. I didn't want to work for a small-town department where opportunities were slim. I wouldn't turn down a job anywhere, but I knew that starting small would mean continuing to test for another, more lucrative department while working at my current post.

After about a year of testing with numerous departments, I finally received the life-changing letter from Broward County telling me I was hired!

And still, that was only the beginning of a very long, arduous process.

THREE

NERVES OF STEEL AND LASER FOCUS

Many people sign up for fire rescue for the commendations and the honors, and those are well deserved, but they're also hard-earned. My hope is to show you what it truly takes to be a firefighter and, if you're considering the profession yourself, to strengthen your resolve to do the personal work required to pursue this noble profession.

STRENGTH is a powerful word indeed, and it has many meanings. You will have to demand and command strength—both mental and physical—to pursue a career in Fire Rescue.

When most people think of firefighters, they think of physical strength, and that's certainly required regardless of your gender or size. But does that mean that everybody who is in shape is capable of becoming a firefighter? Hell, no.

Mental strength is just as important as physical strength, and sometimes more so. If you want to be a firefighter, you need nerves of steel and strength of body, mind, and character. You need to learn to believe in yourself when others doubt you or attempt to sway your chosen path by intimidation, enticement, or threat. You must be strong enough to thrive in spite of the many obstacles thrown your way. It is not my intention to scare you but to prepare you for all the above.

The stares, glares, and whispering will begin on the first day of firefighting boot camp, testing your strength of character and determination. Both men and women will size you up to determine whether they think you'll be a viable competitor or threat to their own job prospects.

The instructors will size you up, too, testing you to see how you react under scrutiny and pressure. The idea is that when an instructor breaks down the group, exposing their weaknesses, fears, and phobias, they will bond faster and more deeply, learning to help each other get through tough days and becoming more confident and resilient. After all, boot camp is like kindergarten compared to the real-life situations you will encounter as a member of the crew.

Stay calm, cool, and focused. Project confidence, even when you're not feeling it. None of them—not your fellow trainees or your instructors—know who you are or what you're made of yet. And you don't know them, either. I learned quickly that the toughest-looking, most intimidating badass can just as easily turn out to be the biggest whiner of all or your best advocate.

Trust me when I tell you that you will learn very quickly who has your back and who will throw you under the bus for their own selfish gain. As a woman in the field, I also learned quickly that some of my colleagues believed strength, courage, tenacity, and resolution could only come in a six-foot male package. That was the case throughout the course of my career, and I know it's still the case today. Some of those colleagues will try and charm you, wanting to get to know you on a more *personal* level, and others will make it clear they think women are better equipped to stay in the kitchen than the firehouse. That is nonsense, of course—just their own insecurities showing. Nonetheless, it takes significant inner strength not to let them get to you.

Fire academy was tough, but I loved every bit of it. To me, passing the state exam and receiving my State of Florida Fire Certificate was a miracle. But if I thought *that* training was hard, boy, was I in for a rude awakening.

The department where I finally got hired had its own five-and-a-half-week boot camp from hell. Eleven of us lucky souls, nine men and two women, were preparing to start this journey together, and if we passed boot camp, we would be probationary recruits, or "probies," for our first year on the job. During boot camp, we would wear stinky, ill-fitting, worn-out gear that different fire departments had donated to the academy. Most of the time, it didn't fit properly, but the instructors just told us to deal with it. Hey, at least it was free. Nowadays recruits must rent the stuff from a company.

Our recruit class consisted of nine men and two women. Knowing how hard it was going to be—and how much harder we'd have to work to prove ourselves—the other female and I made a pact with each other to never cry or whine outside of the confines of the women's bathroom.

And we never did.

She was a couple of years younger than me, but she had experience as a volunteer firefighter in Palm Beach County. She was a strong, fierce triathlete who didn't take shit from anyone, and we figured she would make chief years before any of us did. Although our personalities were very different, I was fortunate to go through boot camp with her. Before fire academy, she had made ends meet working as a waitress and training dolphins at a famous tourist trap in the keys. Hell, both of us were grateful to get a paycheck and a chance at a stable, meaningful career.

She, myself, and one of the guys who got hired with us became close friends. We had all signed up for EMT school at the same academy where we got our fire certifications. The two of them knew each other because they were in the same fire academy class, and I was enrolled in the next one, so it was ironic that the three of us ended up getting hired at the same time.

We started out each day of boot camp with PE, which included basic exercises and running around the fire academy grounds. Then we put on our fire gear, or "bunker gear" as it is commonly called, sometimes adding an air pack, and hustled from station to station performing training tasks. For example, we would chop green telephone poles with a flat-headed ax, then pick up a roll of hose, sling it over our shoulders, and proceed to climb seven flights of stairs, drop the hose, and hit the ground for pushups. Then we'd pick up the hose again and run back down the stairs before dropping it and proceeding to the next task. This might include dragging a hundred-and-fifty-pound dummy to the designated area or carrying a twenty-four-foot ladder to the side of a building, raising it alone, tying the halyard off, and checking the climbing angle at the end. Usually, we did both. We repeated all these exercises many times over, meticulously following a wide range of safety procedures, and all during the sweltering Florida summer. Thank goodness I was in shape before I got started.

In addition to the physical portion of boot camp, there was an enormous amount to learn in the classroom—even beyond what we'd learned at the fire academy. This included the different kinds of fire extinguishers, the ins and outs of building construction, the makeups of different hazardous materials, the nuances of which equipment to use for which kinds of jobs, and so much more. It just got harder and harder as the weeks progressed.

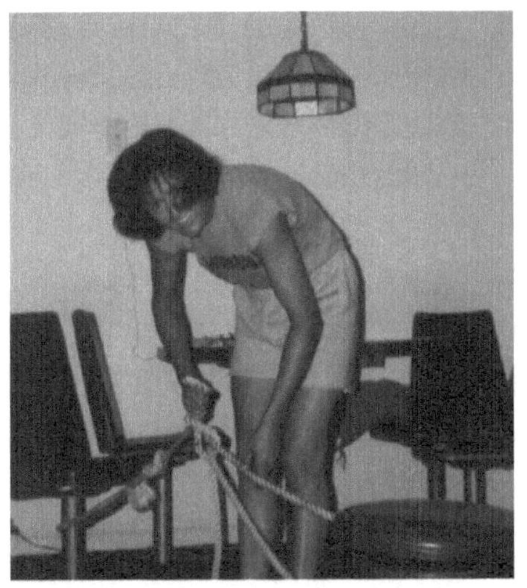

One of the critical skills we had to master was knot tying. We had to learn several different kinds of knots to hoist tools, secure areas, or tie off the halyard on a ladder. But the most important one to learn at the time was a rescue knot, used to extricate a downed firefighter from a building by lowering him or her out of a window and onto a lower balcony or to the ground and out of harm's way. I practiced on my best friend's roommate in their apartment, and he was very good-natured about pretending to be my victim. He and my best friend were roommates, they lived on the first floor, and we would practice with the door and windows open. I can only imagine what the neighbors might have thought when they walked by and saw me bent over him with a large rope in my hand. We always got a good chuckle out of that.

As the training became harder, it was inevitable that somebody would fall out from exhaustion when running. When this happened, the rest of us would pick them up and support them from each side to help them complete the run. But if somebody dared to be late when coming back from lunch, we were far less supportive. In fact, we would give them a whole lot of hate, because their tardiness meant all of us had to run more laps, climb more stairs, or whatever other punishment the training officer could think up—always with a nasty gleam in his eye.

The center of our most critical drills—rescue drills—was the burn building, which consisted of several floors, some set up like residences. The instructors would "smoke it up," reducing our visibility just like a real fire would, and then instruct us to go in and "rescue" dummies or, later, instructors or fellow trainees who were posing as victims.

If we were taking a hose line into the burn building, we learned to hang on to it with a death grip so that if we had to exit in a hurry, we could turn around and follow it out to safety. We also learned how to follow a wall in a left- or right-handed search if we didn't have a hose line to follow. We learned to raise different sized ladders and climb them in full gear and air packs to reach the roof or make entry through a window, sometimes while wearing facemasks and breathing from our self-contained breathing apparatus (SCBA). We learned to slow our breathing to conserve the air in our bottles, which were made of steel back then and heavy as hell. If you couldn't control your breathing, you could easily suck down a thirty-minute bottle in ten minutes. Should you run out of air in those days, you had to unhook the hose from your tank and stick it into your bunker coat or your glove and quickly make it to the exit for fresh air.

We learned about using different tools to extend our reach when looking for victims, feeling for bodies underneath furniture and in cabinets, closets, bathrooms, or in the small spaces where children and pets tend to hide. We learned how to recognize when to go into a building to put the fire out and when we needed to fight it defensively because it wasn't safe to enter.

But perhaps most importantly, we learned to stay calm under pressure. All kinds of scary, mock situations were thrown at us, pushing us, building our self-confidence and dependence upon each other, and testing our temperament under intense pressure.

All of this shows you why training and being in great physical shape is paramount. I was fortunate to come into the service already fit. I was a runner, I could jump rope for thirty minutes or more, and I could do all the pushups and sit-ups I was asked to do. But still, these drills pushed me to my limits.

The most difficult, to me, was the maze, a required evolution where you entered the burn building with zero visibility and no flashlights. You chose a right or left search pattern, feeling the wall and checking the floor in front of you with a tool to make sure it was solid. Then, the instructors would throw all kinds of hazards or unpredictable situations at you and your partner. Sometimes you would come to a dead-end and have to figure out how to find a way out. In these cases, I worked hard not to panic, because I certainly didn't want to run out of air. I'd feel everywhere for a blocked window or maybe a small opening to a stairwell to ascend or descend, being careful not to fall into an opening in the floor.

Sometimes the evolutions included very tight openings we had to crawl through or drag ourselves through on our bellies, lowering ourselves feet first or pulling ourselves up. Sometimes this required removing our air packs—and sometimes even our helmets—and pushing them through first, all the while still on air.

This training drill was essential to introduce us to the real-life hazards that could get us hurt, end our careers, or kill us and our crews if we weren't diligent. I understood its importance, but nonetheless, I hated the maze. I would get myself all worked up about it, but I was always able to suck it up and get through it. And this was before escape rooms were invented for fun.

The biggest reason I was able to push through the maze—and any other challenge the training or the real-world calls threw at me—was because of the incredible confidence I had in my colleagues. Because no matter what else we had to do to make it through, the most important thing was maintaining constant communication and trust with our partners. Once, while going through a maze drill with two other guys, I managed to fall through a hole in the floor, dislodging my helmet in the process. (Thank goodness there'd been a mattress placed on the ground for that very reason.) I was shaken, but it definitely taught me to use my tools to feel in front of me for a solid floor. One of the instructors that particular day was very calm. He reassured me that I was fine and directed me to finish the evolution with my partners. A few years later, we'd become friends, and whenever we ran into each other or worked together, he would tease me about falling through that hole in the maze.

My instincts and good common sense were usually on point, but I never lost sight of the fact that I was very fortunate to work with men who were seasoned, calm, and confident in my abilities. Although I never claimed to be the best or the smartest firefighter, I worked with some extraordinary ones. That, along with training, continuing education, and experience, was key to my success.

One of our instructors was an old-school chief whom I really respected. We called him "The Legend," and I would later have the honor of working in his battalion. But in training, he loved to throw buckets of mineral spirits onto bales of hay in the burn building before we entered and light them up! His motto was that, if your helmet wasn't black or melted after you came out of there, it wasn't hot enough. One of our other training exercises was to free-climb a rope hanging from the roof of an old, falling-down, one-story number that was about to be condemned, walk across the narrow open walkway, then exit the other side via an old metal ladder. This was dicey, and he usually had us do it after we were physically spent, but he knew that sometimes, in the real world, we'd have to keep going when we had nothing left. The Legend would train us all day long, never seeming to get tired, and when the day ended, he would gladly drink a couple of cold beers with us before heading home.

As time went on, different evolutions would be added to our training. For example, sometimes we'd have to jog in full gear, running shoes, and air pack two-and-a-half miles to the police academy (chanting military chants the whole way, of course), then go through the police officer training obstacle course and jog back to the fire academy, where we'd do walking handstands around barrels. I know it sounds absurd, but I just loved it, all of it. The sweatier, the better. For me, failure was not an option. My confidence, strength, and willpower grew, and I excelled. I felt unstoppable.

The instructor who led us during those runs to the police academy was a brilliant, handsome, and charismatic man. He would jog next to us, chanting with us while smoking a cigarette. He made it look so easy, even as they got more and more difficult as time went on. Still, even at their hardest, these training runs were nothing compared to the real-life emergency situations I would encounter on shift. We had to complete one last evolution, and it lasted the whole day ending with us going through the maze to find a hidden, colored chip.

All eleven of us made it!

A couple of days after that last evolution, eleven smiling, proud, brand-new probies, nine men and two women, raised our right hands and took the oath, swearing to protect the lives and property of the citizens of Broward County. On that day, all we could focus on were our bright futures, our regular paychecks, and the cold beers that were in order after the ceremony that evening.

I have always said I hit the lottery twice. That day was the first time, and the second time was when I met my future husband. (I must admit that I didn't like to see him at first, because he was responsible for delivering the green telephone poles that we recruits had to chop. Little did I know that he was also sizing up the group to parlay the information to the guys on duty so they had an idea of who we were and who might be on their shifts. But more on him later.)

Finally, I had a career that I could feel good about. I was proud to know I was in a position to make a difference to people who needed help. This job was going to be exciting and, most importantly, satisfying. Never again would I be bored to tears at a desk or depressed on Friday nights knowing Monday was just around the corner.

With the boot camp behind me, I was eager to celebrate and cut loose a bit with my new colleagues. But The Legend had an idea that had us *really* letting loose. The guys knew I also had my cosmetology license, so The Legend suggested that I color his white hair bright red. A couple of other guys raised their hands to have theirs done, too, so I complied. I gave them short buzz cuts first so they wouldn't have much trouble growing it out. For most of the guys, the scheme went perfectly. They enjoyed their red hair for a few days and then shaved it back off in time to look respectable for shift. But The Legend's hair just turned purple, and it took quite a while to grow back out. He was good-humored about it, but to me, it was further validation that firefighting, not hairdressing, was my true calling.

Cosmetology shenanigans over, it was time for all eleven of us to pick a folded piece of paper out of a hat to determine what shift we would be assigned to: A for Alpha, B for Bravo, or C for Charlie. The rumor was that A shift was the best, B shift was okay, and C shift had all the hard-asses and losers. Whichever shift we landed, we'd work twenty-four hours on and have forty-eight hours off, with a rotating shift off every four weeks called a Kelly Day. (Whoever Kelly is, we would all like to thank him if we ever get the chance!) When it was my turn, I dug out a piece of white paper and unfolded it to find the holy grail: A shift.

Yes!

Reflecting now, I know that whether a shift is "good" or not is more about the crews you work with than the actual shift. There were plenty of capable firefighters assigned to each of the three shifts, as well as a few idiots to spread around. Still, I have to say, I always did prefer A shift.

With my new probie status and my A-shift slip in hand, I felt a surge of pride in my chest. That kind of pride is what I wish for every new firefighter upon finally receiving that T-shirt that says, "Firefighter" or "Probie Firefighter" and embarking on this meaningful career.

Pride, self-respect, self-esteem, and most of all, self-sufficiency should all become part of your identity when you put on that shirt for the very first time. You are now a part of an exclusive club for life. Don't take it for granted, because this is a noble calling, no matter how big or small the department that hired you. You made the important decision to go down this path, and you're now in the throes of beginning your probationary year.

It's up to you now to decide how to conduct yourself, and believe me, appearances matter. My suggestion is to walk tall, reflecting that pride you feel. I have seen people show up for shift with the nastiest looking uniforms: ill-fitting, wrinkled T-shirts with holes or stains, scuffed-up boots, and pants that look like they've never been ironed. Can you imagine what the public thinks when they see a firefighter getting out of the rig looking like that? Nobody likes to see their beloved firefighters, or "heroes" as you will undoubtedly be called, looking like vagabonds.

It seems like common sense to me, but not everyone gets it, and I've seen both students and professionals show up looking every kind of bedraggled you could think of. Once, when I was an officer, a student reported to my station to ride with me. He was late, and he was looking very sloppy, so I read him the riot act. "Buy a damn belt, pull your hair back, buy a watch so you can take patient vitals, and show up on time, for God's sake," I told him.

This kid had already put me in a bad mood, so thank goodness I was wrapping up my shift when the next rocket scientist showed up to ride. He was on the verge of being late, and like clockwork, a medical call came in right at shift change. The off-going crews scurried to grab our gear off the truck as the oncoming crews were throwing theirs on.

As the countdown began, the student ran to the truck and hopped on to respond with the oncoming crew. Well, apparently, his bladder was about to burst, and of course, he hadn't arrived early enough to take care of that before shift. They handled the call, transferred the patient to the ER, and were enroute back to the station when this guy—who never told anybody he needed to pee and didn't have the sense to go at the hospital or relieve himself into a red medical waste bag—proceeded to relieve himself on the floor of the rescue truck. You can only imagine the fury that ensued. Let's just say the student disappeared, never to complete his education as a paramedic. His bad judgment had cost him his career. Crazy stuff, but I always say truth is stranger than fiction.

Don't confuse pride with arrogance, but always take the time to look—and act—professional. So what if you have to fill out the proper paperwork to exchange your ratty old stuff or use some off-duty personal time to handle your wardrobe? You worked damn hard to get here, and you owe it to yourself to look as good as you feel.

Have pride in yourself and in the career that you have chosen to be a part of. You'll feel better, and people will notice.

FOUR

THE CORRECT TERM FOR A FEMALE FIREFIGHTER: "FIREFIGHTER"

It made me wonder what they thought I should look like. After all, not all of the men looked like the traditional calendar boys. Just like in real life, some were handsome and in great shape, and some were not. I do believe that we have a certain image to uphold, but a firefighter's skill and worth aren't connected to his *or her* looks. "I am not a man and never wanted to be one," I would tell the guys, "but I am part of this crew."

My first night on shift, the battalion chief who had jogged and chanted with our probie class during boot camp gave me his private room, a coveted perk for an officer. Poor Chief; too bad he didn't know that he was violating the code, because he was severely chastised for it. He was a total badass, but he treated me with respect, and he knew I was a capable, determined firefighter. He just wasn't accustomed to having a woman on the crew, and he was trying to be polite. But he knew better than anyone that, in the firehouse, everyone is treated the same, male or female.

So, from then on, I had to sleep in the matchbox-sized bunkroom with the other two blue shirts on my shift, who had a couple of years of seniority on me. The room was so small that the three twin beds, each against a wall, almost touched each other. One of the guys insisted on sleeping in his bikini briefs, and it pissed me off to no end at first because I thought he was testing me and being disrespectful. Little did I know then just how important he would become in my life.

Reflecting on that memory now, my annoyance seems silly, in part because I'd never been much for modesty. Growing up in Florida, running around town in a bathing suit and shorts, or maybe a sheer cover-up and flip-flops, is a way of life. And when you are young and muscular, showing your body in a respectful way just seems natural. Besides, when I was modeling, I frequently had to change clothes at a shoot, with someone holding up a towel if I was lucky. But more importantly, I quickly learned just how insignificant it is seeing your co-workers in their underwear, jumping out of bed to get into work pants or bunker pants and boots, and running to the truck to respond when the bell goes off in the middle of the night.

Besides my friend from boot camp and me, there was one other woman who'd been hired about the same time we were. She was a trapeze artist—beautiful, fit, and fierce. I found out much later from a fellow firefighter that the officers didn't know what to do with us when it came to sleeping accommodations, bathrooms, etc. (Hence, the offer of the private room on that first night.) But ultimately, the three of us, each on a different shift, were treated as equals, and the requirements were never adjusted for our gender. That would become crucial as time went on, and the firehouse telephone/telegraph pipeline started.

There was one woman, a true pioneer that I must mention. She was a volunteer firefighter with the West Broward Volunteer Fire District #27. When all of Broward Counties Fire Districts merged in September 1980, she was recruited to work as a secretary for one of the Chiefs. However, she remained on the payroll as an active firefighter. She was well respected, but sadly she died of cancer soon after retirement.

None of the members hired after the merge were required to attend a twelve week orientation or bootcamp. My group of eleven lucky soles were the first. Prior to that, staffing was bare bones with only one or two on an engine.

Unfortunately, not all the women involved in the fire department were as upstanding as this secretary. I'd heard stories of women who'd been hired and let go during their probationary periods because they were unable to live up to the firehouse standards. One of them was almost there—a week out from getting off of probation—before she got drunk in a bar, challenged somebody to a fight, and got pulled over for a DUI. I don't know if she was just trying to behave like "one of the guys" or if she felt she had something to prove. Regardless, she was quickly fired.

Another woman who had been hired before me was looking for a hookup. I used to run into her when I was testing to get hired for different departments, usually when I was outside getting ready for the physical agility exercises. She called most of the fire instructors by their first names, which seemed kind of strange at first but made perfect sense later on. During my first shift, another guy and I were driven around to different stations to meet the other crews. One of the oldest stations had Murphy beds in the room that served as a dayroom when they were up, and it was the bunkroom at night when they were pulled down out of the wall. We walked into one station in the middle of the day, and guess who was laying on it with the officer on duty. You guessed it: Miss Too-Familiar. She found herself pregnant and left shortly thereafter.

I don't say all this to put my fellow women down. Lord knows there were men in the departments behaving badly, too. But as women, right or wrong, we had to work harder to prove we were up to the job. I was busting my ass to earn my place in my dream career. Regardless of the reasoning, though, my two female colleagues and I were it. It was up to us to prove to the guys that a woman could absolutely have what it takes to be a firefighter. My favorite battalion chief, the one who threw the buckets of mineral spirits onto bales of hay when I was going through boot camp, sternly warned me about a particular officer who had invited me to one of his frequent house parties. He told me to never go near his house or parties under any circumstances. Although the chief was old, known as a wild man, and loved women, he was wise and treated me like a daughter. He told me something I had already learned a long time ago: that you are judged by the company you keep.

I am proud of the two women I got hired with and of all those who came afterward. Even today, firefighting isn't a common career choice for most women. There are still a lot of misconceptions about those of us who have joined the force. When I took fire classes for my associate's degree at the college closer to my home, I constantly had to explain to guys in my class that yes, I had been hired by a large, urban department, and no, they didn't lower the requirements for me or any of the other women. I encountered men outside of work who were dismissive of me when I traveled to other places on vacation, and when asked what I did for a living, I proudly told them I was a firefighter. I felt like a puppy and waited for them to pet me on the top of my head, saying, "Oh, really? You're a firefighter?" It pissed me off, but I knew that some men had horrible experiences watching women be treated differently on the job than me. The New York City Fire Department had supposedly lowered its standards in the 1970s so it could feel a quota of females and minorities, and many people assumed that our department had done the same. But that wasn't my experience. In my opinion, it is a mistake to change the requirements for anyone, regardless of size or gender. It is insulting, creates animosity, and frankly, can be dangerous for everyone involved.

But just because the standards weren't lowered for my fellow women and me doesn't mean we were never treated differently. Sometimes it was because our male colleagues couldn't imagine we were physically capable of doing the job. People used to question whether or not I could drag a man out of a building by myself. Well, the answer is that we work as a crew, and there are plenty of men who can't drag a man out of a building by themselves either. Technique, training, and experience all come into play no matter the situation. And besides, in training, I had successfully dragged a 150-pound dummy at least fifty feet and dragged firefighters in full bunker gear and air packs out of the burn building. I was confident in my abilities, and I knew I'd never be facing that situation alone. In the fire department, we are a crew that depends on each other. We go in together, and we leave together.

Other times, some of the guys would want to help me check the truck and equipment, making sure I'd maintained the saws, jaws of life, generators, and other heavy equipment correctly, keeping it in good working order and ready to be used if needed. I would tell the guys who volunteered to help that we each had our jobs to do, so we should leave each other alone and focus on doing them. I understood their ingrained chivalry, but I knew better than to accept it. I would ask for advice or help if I needed it, just like any firefighter should, male or female. But until then, I would be self-sufficient.

There was plenty of hazing in the station, too, though most of that was entirely gender-neutral. All the probies got picked on equally. Again, they wanted to freeze my blue class A shirt. For example, there was a tradition where the more senior firefighters folded up the probies' T-shirts, badge and nametag perfectly in place, and then stuck them in the freezer. Sometimes they ran them up the flagpole located in front of the station for us to find later.

The two guys I worked with would try to pull funny tricks on me. Once they removed the castor wheels from my bed and replaced them with pencils, adding aerosol cans so when I plopped down on my bed to go to sleep, the pencils would break, and they would go off. Well, the joke was on them. I was so light that the aerosol cans never went off because the pencils never broke, and I had a great night of sleep. I woke up to see both of them staring at me with shit-eating grins, shaking their heads in fake disgust, and calling me "the princess and the pea."

The guys also wanted to turn off the hot water in the bathroom out in the bay where I showered—and they'd done it to plenty of the guys—but my wonderful lieutenant quickly put the kibosh to that, and under no circumstances would he allow them to enter the bathroom while I was in there. (So, I guess one "rule" was bent a little bit for me.) Then, they wanted to spray me with a fire extinguisher when I came out of the bathroom once, and again, my lieutenant said absolutely not.

The firehouse has certainly evolved over the years, and I can't help but remember the different chiefs I worked with under their command or had contact with in my early days on the job. The statute of limitations has run out by now, and many of the chiefs I worked with are long retired or dead, so I don't think they'll mind if I share a couple of stories. One chief gave all his crew—including me and one other female firefighter—a choice on payday: In order to get our checks, we could either give blood or head to the local strip club where the guys went to let off steam, spending their money on booze and dancers. The funny thing was, the other woman and I both agreed to get our paychecks at the strip club instead of having to give blood. We would walk in and join the guys, chief included, at a long table, unfazed by the beautiful dancers. I was never bothered much by that, though looking back on it and realizing that my male colleagues were just handed their paychecks with no hoops to jump through, it makes me glad times have changed. We both thought, *So what if they are naked? We have bills to pay and just want our paychecks.* The dancers, on their part, probably thought fire department payday was like shooting fish in a barrel. They played it up whenever we were there, including treating us women to private lap dances. The dancers were beautiful, and we took the opportunity to find out what kind of lotions they used to keep their skin so soft—you know, typical girl talk. They were nice to us, and we to them. After all, everybody needs a job.

These behaviors—playing pranks on us, making us jump through hoops to get our paychecks—were inappropriate and obnoxious, but it was all in the spirit of good fun, signaling that us younger firefighters, men and women alike, were part of the group. Fortunately, I never had to experience the hurtful, nasty, gender-inspired tricks that some of the men in other departments played on their female colleagues. One woman told me the guys she worked with shit in her bunker boots, nailed her locker shut, and refused to allow her to eat with them at the table. This terrible, disgusting behavior would never be tolerated in today's world, but back then, it happened more often than not. That wasn't hazing—it was cruel. In what world is that kind of behavior considered okay? It was also especially stupid of these men, given that, any minute, they could be depending on those women for their safety during an emergency call.

While I'm grateful that I never found myself in those overtly hostile situations, I did encounter my fair share of men who just didn't want a woman working with them no matter how competent they might be, and some of them would try to undermine me. Some were young guys trying to push their bravado and, as I climbed the ranks, others were pissed that I was an officer and they hadn't passed the tests or taken classes that would've qualified them for promotions.

I knew full well that I was joining something of a "boys' club," and for the most part, it didn't bother me. It's interesting, looking back, that I chose this mostly male profession, because although I had grown up never showing it, I was scared to death of men for much of my young life. I'd been molested at the age of six by a neighbor. This was only discovered when my oldest sister Carolyn, who was sixteen years older than me, came to visit. She was bathing me in the old metal tub, and she discovered some very bad stuff showing up on my private parts. Furious, she informed our parents of what was happening, and they put a stop to it. The chain of events that followed, however, was just as traumatic. Having to go to court at six years old and sit in front of a jury while reliving the events was frightening, to say the least. And, unfortunately, it was never spoken of again, because my family was of the mindset that if you don't talk about it, you can forget about it. This had a huge effect on how I would interact with men for years to come, but a very wise friend eventually pushed me into counseling, which was the best thing I ever did. I would think about it from time to time, wondering how in the hell could someone molest a little child, but by the time I had joined the fire service, I had worked through enough of the trauma to understand that I had met and become friends with some truly exceptional men whom I trusted completely whether it was on the job or in my personal life.

When I first started working, I would see pictures of naked women taped to the inside of some of the guys' lockers. It never fazed me as long as they weren't hanging the pictures in the bunkroom or anywhere else in plain sight. I figured, who cares?

I did draw the line, though, at another firefighter's habit of watching porn on the living room TV while he was on duty. I told him I didn't care what he did on his own time, but that wouldn't fly in the station—whether there were women around or not.

I think most of these men simply took for granted the idea that I was a "prissy" girl who could be easily cowed. I believed in taking good care of myself and was perhaps even a little vane. I knew that I looked good in those days. One time, when I was off duty and walking around the shopping center next to the salon, where I lived in the taxpayer above, I heard a male voice say, "Can I see your ID?" I was wearing a black minidress and flip-flops, and I was lean and tanned. Imagine my surprise when I turned around to see a police officer sitting behind the wheel of his patrol car, which had pulled up alongside me with his window rolled down. I said, "Excuse me?" He repeated, "Do you have an ID?" now sounding like a jerk. I asked, "Why do you want to see it?" wondering what in the world he thought I'd done. He was acting like kind of a jerk, and I was eager to see his reaction when I handed him my official county firefighter ID. Sure enough, his face turned beet-red, and his self-satisfied smirk melted away. Once he collected himself, he politely said, "I am so sorry, miss, but I've been getting reports of a working girl in the neighborhood."

Really, you asshole? I thought but didn't say it. *Do I look like a hooker to you?* Must have been the short black dress. I must admit, I looked good. (In hindsight, I wish I had refused and let him put me in cuffs and haul my ass to jail. What fun it would have been to call my battalion chief to come and get me and watch the fireworks.)

Although I loved fashion, took care of myself, and enjoyed looking good on my time off, I was anything but prissy. I never wore more than minimal makeup on shift—I just put on sunscreen, did my eyebrows, and braided my hair so I could tuck it up under my helmet. Five minutes and done. That said, I did come in with some elevated expectations of just how "put-together" a female firefighter could get. One day, since I had, at that point, some change in my pocket, I decided to get acrylic nails and have them painted bright red. Hell, they were expensive. My natural ones had always been a soft, peeling mess, but acrylics were a luxury I could not afford prior to getting hired. Well, one day, I walked into the station and sat down at the community table for coffee before my shift started. I proudly held up my hands, displaying my new, long, bright-red nails for all to see. "Aren't they beautiful?" I asked the guys. They looked up from their newspapers and their breakfast plates and laughed. "Are you kidding me?" one of them said. "Yes, they're pretty, but just wait until you start the K12 saw this morning. They'll be history. You can't work with those things, but good luck."

Well, damn it, they were right. Most of those nails snapped right off when I was pulling the cord to start the K12 saw. Shit! All that money down the drain, and they looked even worse than before. The bright-red polish made my ragged nail-tips look like bloody stumps. Okay, geniuses, lesson learned. I had to soak my nails in acetone to remove them. It was an expensive lesson in vanity, and I guess I did deserve some ribbing for that.

The prejudices didn't come only from inside the fire station, either. Some of the guys' wives were upset when they learned there was a female firefighter working side by side with their husbands and possibly sleeping in the same room. I thought it was a little sad that these women were so jealous. Had they bothered to come into the station to introduce themselves, I think they would've realized they had nothing to worry about. Some of them even had the audacity to call us whores and to try to forbid their husbands from working with us. I would just shake my head when I heard things like this. Their husbands weren't going to lose their hard-fought bids because of us, no matter how rare it was to see a woman on a firetruck in 1987.

I did understand their insecurities. I knew what it was like to have a boyfriend or husband who was a firefighter. I could see how just seeing the way people responded to them with such admiration might ignite some fear that their female colleagues would do the same. But I wasn't looking, thank you very much, and the last thing on my mind was the idea of getting involved with a married man. As often as possible, I genuinely befriended my colleagues' wives. I wanted them to know there was nothing to worry about—and besides, being around smelly men all day, I could use a few more females in my life!

I learned to work with men who were from a different generation, and I tried not to judge them too harshly as long as they weren't disrespectful. Some were a little gruff and rough around the edges, but women firefighters were a new concept they would just have to get used to. Besides, my father was born in 1917, the last of nineteen kids, and he cussed and talked gruff enough to give me an edge. I was hard to shock. But for the most part, even these older guys treated me with respect, though were no doubt curious and probably dumbfounded that I'd chosen this career. The crustiest old-timers seemed to give me the benefit of the doubt. Still, they saw how hard I worked, and that was enough for them.

Despite the sidelong glances, frequent skepticism, and occasional mistreatment, my female colleagues and I were all the buzz. The word out in the field was that we were tough, strong, competent women who could do the job. We were young, fit, and attractive, and we all held our own, whether we were checking equipment or on the scene of a fire. We were grown women who had worked our asses off to get our state fire certificates, to test with different departments and get hired, to make it through our boot camps, and finally, to be on shift, earning our paychecks.

I have to acknowledge, too, that being female wasn't the only reason for a firefighter to be discriminated against. My best friend on the department was a gay man who'd been hired with me and the other woman firefighter. The three of us went to EMT school together. He was handsome, masculine, and smart. He had a friend who was very rich, owned a yacht, had a house on Fort Lauderdale beach, and drove a Rolls Royce. He could borrow the yacht anytime he wished so when he asked us if we wanted to go for a boat ride down the intracoastal waterway, stop at the bar, get lunch and a drink, we said hell, yes! The fire service wasn't very open to gay or lesbian people at that time. He wanted to excel in his career and become a paramedic, because he loved helping people. Unfortunately for him, the fire service wasn't very open to homosexuality at that point, and other men, including a couple of chiefs he worked with, shunned him and made his life a living hell. He ended up quitting, and he died tragically from AIDS a couple of years later. The other woman and I were brokenhearted, and we never forgot the cruelty he endured when all he ever wanted to do was save lives.

In lighter memories, I must talk about another exceptional man I worked with, who remains one of my good friends today. He is also gay and was very open about it when he worked for our department, seemingly unfazed by the neanderthal ignorance that was rampant back then. He was a driver-engineer when I floated into his station one shift. The station was an old, two-story building with a tiny bunk room, including a small, separate quarters for the officer, with the kitchen and the only bathroom located downstairs off the bay. I was in the bathroom getting dressed that morning when there was a knock on the door. (Since it was the only bathroom in the station, I always tried to get up before the guys to get ready and remove my things before they got up.) Imagine my surprise when I opened the door to see him standing there with his big blue eyes, gorgeous smile, and perfect body—wearing the skimpiest briefs I had ever seen. "Good morning," he said brightly, then informed me that if I hadn't ever seen a man in his underwear before, it was time. Well, I had seen a couple of men in their underwear before, but he wore his with confidence and pride, so it made me smile knowing he meant nothing sexual or lecherous about it, and while the little prank may have been inappropriate—especially by today's standards—I couldn't help but laugh.

Given all the shenanigans we endured—of the good, bad, and ugly varieties—it now seems fitting to me that the very first fire that I put out was at a "shit house" (the correct terminology is a "Porta John") that some asshole had decided to light up in a local park. The guys I was on duty with teased me unmercifully, but I thought, *Who cares? Just put the damn thing out.* So I grabbed the nozzle and did it. I'd grown up using a pot behind a curtain just off of the kitchen, for Christ's sake. My poor, disabled mother had to take it outside to empty it into the outhouse, regardless of the weather. So this wasn't nearly as disgusting to me as the boys assumed. Rather, I took it as a sign from my mother that my days of getting metaphorically shit on were over.

I can honestly say my feelings did get hurt sometimes, and maybe that is a flaw of mine, but I was old enough and had worked enough jobs where the boss was a creepy son of a bitch that I'd learned to know what to let get under my skin and what to let go of. One of my many experiences with lecherous men occurred when I was only twenty-four and my two other female cohorts were twenty-two. It was an office job, and we were just trying to pay the bills. Our illustrious boss, who was in his thirties, would come in and rub his hand across our backs to "see if we were wearing bras." And he would ask us to lift up our skirts to see if we were wearing underwear. We never gave him the satisfaction, but in those days, you didn't raise a stink about things like that; instead, we shrugged it off and continued to work. So, by the time I was hired by the fire department, I had a pretty strong will to not let ignorant, insecure men keep me from fulfilling my desire to have a long career in the fire service.

And even when that will wasn't quite enough, I had internalized these two pieces of advice from two veteran fire chiefs, reminding me that I belonged in the department as much as any man:

The first one, an old-time New York Firefighter who came down to Fort Lauderdale on vacation, had said, "I don't give a shit if you're yellow, black, purple, female, or otherwise if you can do the job. That is what matters the most." I took his comments to heart and proceeded from there.

The second was a crusty, old chief who told me there's a place on the fireground for everyone. If you're a big, tall, musclebound guy, you'll be using your size and ability for the jobs that require it. On the other hand, if you're small in stature, like I was, climbing and crawling into small spaces will likely be your specialty. Sure enough, I don't remember how many times I would have to crawl through a small window when we showed up for a medical call and the door was locked. This is why diversity of skills, abilities, and even sizes are assets—not detriments—to a fire crew. The best officers I knew recognized this, and they knew that, just like every man on the crew, I brought my own set of strengths to the table.

FIVE

A JOB TO BE PROUD OF

The department that I worked for was young in both its members and history. It definitely wasn't steeped in history like FDNY or Chicago Fire. Broward County had originally been composed of volunteer departments from different municipalities, and it had become a professional paid entity around the late 1970s or early '80s. Our department was on a shoestring budget when I was hired in the 1980s, but as time went on, and different administrations came and went, more resources, new equipment, and the latest medications became available. We even had non-rebreather masks for animals and big nets to rescue ducks that had fallen into storm drains. But when I was hired, we didn't have any of that yet, and I credit the department's relative youth as one of the reasons I was accepted. Most of the guys were young and, though a few were seasoned volunteers who'd worked together for years, everyone on the force was new to being paid professionals. Whatever the reasons, I was proud to be there. I was focused and driven by a calling that spoke to me in a way that no other job had before. And I loved the busy stations. Some were so damn busy, you ran on pure adrenaline, which was fulfilling to me, because I'd learned I get bored easily. I loved not knowing what kind of shift I would have or what kind of calls I would respond to. Although it was nice to work a slow shift so we could eat, train, work out, and maybe sleep through the night, I couldn't stand that mundane routine for long.

The fire service is paramilitary by design, and I discovered that I loved the discipline, the structure, and the formality. Here's an overview of how that structure worked. The rank structure starts with firefighter-paramedic at the bottom, then moves up to chauffer or driver-engineer, lieutenant, and captain. The battalion chiefs are responsible for multiple fire stations and personnel within their district. The captain is in charge of the station, and the lieutenant is in charge of the members assigned to a specific truck, be it engine or rescue. When a call comes in, the officer who is the first on scene takes command of the situation, and once a higher-ranking officer arrives, they assume command. If the scene requires multiple companies, then the battalion chief will arrive and take command. The rank structure continues up the chain, depending on the seriousness of the emergency and the units and personnel needed.

And the crew members, themselves, aren't the only person-nel needed. There are units on scene to rehab the firefighters and monitor their vitals if needed, others to fill air bottles, and if it is an extensive scene, there are replacement crews on standby and someone ready to address nutrition needs. Sometimes a cold pizza was a welcome sight when the incident lasted for hours or days. This is called organized chaos at its best.

Large cities such as New York or Portland usually have more resources and can put a lot of people on the scene of an emergency call, but standard operating procedures in the department I worked in were to staff four people on a ladder truck, three on an engine, and two on a rescue truck (unless a city paid to have a third). The biggest firehouses I was in charge of as captain had a ladder truck with four people, an engine with three people, and two rescue trucks with three on each.

When the tones went off to signal an emergency call, they would almost give you a heart attack. They were so loud and shrill, they could peel the paint off the walls, and they would surely wake the dead. We'd get dressed in a hurry, nearly knocking each other over as we ran to the truck with dragon breath, sleep lines on our faces, wild hair going in all directions, and adrenaline pumping.

If the crew was stellar, we made the best of whatever came our way. In the fire service, we go in together and leave together, and I took that rule to heart on every call, no matter the circumstance. One firefighter who I'd known years before I was hired eventually began working at Broward County. By the time we reconnected, I was an acting driver engineer, and we'd work together once I became a lieutenant as well. He told me once that he knew I would never leave him alone, no matter what situation we found ourselves in. That is a profound statement, and I felt the same way about him. I breathed a sigh of relief whenever he was my driver for a shift. Unfortunately, he also died a young death from cancer, leaving his wife behind, as well as a son who proudly followed in his footsteps.

Not long after my probation started, a call came in for a huge brush fire in the southwestern area of the county, very close to a huge retirement condo community. Departments from all over the county pitched in to ensure the flames didn't reach the condos, which could have been disastrous. There was a spare engine housed in our station; the same battalion chief who'd given me his room on my first shift told me to get in. We were assisting at the brush fire, he said, and I was driving.

Are you kidding me? I was shaking in my boots as I climbed up into the seat, but I mustered all my bravado and said, "Yes, sir, let's go!" It was a terrible fire. There were heavy winds that day, large melaleuca trees were exploding from the heat, and the fire seemed to be creating its own weather. The closer we got, the less visibility we had. There were multiple units responding, and it was hard to make out the flashing lights in the smoke as we tried not to run into each other. Another engine that had responded with us went off-road trying to get closer to the fire and came very close to getting stuck. The radio was blowing up with requests for rescue units to respond to the retirement community for respiratory and other medical problems caused by the thick smoke.

In spite of all the chaos, the battalion chief was calm, and it didn't seem to faze him whatsoever that I, a brand-new probie, was his driver. We managed to put out the fire before it reached the retirement community, and my confidence soared after that call. I was thankful that the battalion chief trusted me when I had no experience.

A few shifts later at the same station, I was given another task. Like that battalion chief, my first lieutenant was more confident in my abilities than I was. He was a good guy, had two daughters he adored, and a wife who was an incredible paramedic and always very kind to me. Shortly after the brush fire, he asked me to pick up the fire truck from the motor pool and drive it back to the station by myself. I panicked for a minute. I drove a little red Volkswagen Beetle, and I knew how to drive a stick shift as well as a manual with a shifter on the column, but a big fire engine? And with no officer riding with me for support? Those engines were massive, with no rear-view mirrors, and driving them was incredibly intimidating— at least, the first couple of times. I quickly got used to it and even began to enjoy it.

The best part of driving the fire truck, to me, was watching people's faces when they realized a woman was behind the wheel. This was rare in 1987. I absolutely loved to see the look on little girls' faces when they saw me riding backward on the old, open-cab engines or, later in my career, driving engines or ladder or tanker trucks or, as an officer, sitting in the front passenger seat, mic in my hand, talking on the radio. I always smiled at waved at the kids we passed—especially the little girls.

Yes, I took incredible pride in my career—a pride I hadn't even known was possible. And sharing that pride with others made it grow even stronger.

• • •

After six months at my first assignment, I was evaluated and tested for proficiency. I passed and was deemed ready to move on to a different station, where I would be re-evaluated after six months. The first year of employment is tough because, as a probie, you have no right to an opinion on anything. If you are smart, you keep your mouth shut. If you're doing it right, you're the first person setting the table for dinner, clearing the lunch or dinner dishes, and cleaning the station after dinner—including the bathrooms. Brownie points if you have the coffee going before anybody else is up in the mornings. This shows initiative and respect for your crew and your "home." When you're on duty, you show up ready to work at least fifteen minutes prior to starting the shift. By the time your officer arrives, you're already outside in the bay, checking out every piece of equipment on the truck—and you've memorized where everything is kept. Nothing pisses off an officer more than giving you an order on scene and then hearing the banging of the compartment doors because you don't know which compartment the tool they asked for is in. Trust me: Your evaluation will reflect that disappointment. I was thrilled to pass that first evaluation, because I was more than ready to spread my wings, gain more experience, and work with different crews.

My new station, like all the stations in the department, had a schedule of duties that were to be done each day of the week. Monday was truck day. Though all the trucks and equipment were checked daily, we did more thorough inspections on Mondays. This meant crawling underneath to check fluid levels and spot possible leaks, running the pump, and verifying that the fans, tools, ladders, and everything else on the trucks were working correctly. I would put on an old jumpsuit, goggles, and gloves and get the creeper out to crawl underneath the trucks to check for loose hoses, fluids, or any abnormalities that could potentially create a problem. Geared up, I'd grab a wrench and an orange box light, and down I would go, laying on this uncomfortable, wood-slatted contraption with wheels. It was not a comfortable position to be in, and I was not mechanically inclined (I'd never changed the oil or a tire on my own vehicle), so this was trial by fire, but I sucked it up and got through it. My inspiration was my brother, Gary, who could take apart engines—carburetors being his specialty—when he was just sixteen years old. He loved to fix up old cars, and he always had 1957 Chevrolets that he'd race on Friday or Saturday nights. I'm sure he would've laughed at me if he'd seen me in my grease-covered jumpsuit holding a wrench. But I like to think he would've been proud, too.

After the trucks were checked out and our beds were made, the most important conversation took place: food. What was for lunch and dinner, who was going to cook, and how much was it going to cost? I often got a little bit annoyed walking through the grocery store to buy food for our twenty-four-hour shift. Some people assumed, incorrectly, that our food bill was paid for on the taxpayer dime, and many of them did not hesitate to give their opinions as we loaded our cart with food.

More than once we would get a call while shopping, and we'd have to leave the cart with the cashier, begging her to hang onto it so we could retrieve it after the call. Sometimes they'd put it in the cooler for us, but sometimes when we got back a couple of hours later, the food had been restocked and we'd have to start all over again, hoping to finish and pay before the next call came in.

Tuesday might be makeup day, which covered anything that didn't get done on Monday or had been left hanging from other days' to-do lists, and Wednesday was station GI day, when we scrubbed everything from top to bottom, especially the kitchen. Thursday was lawn day, and in the old days, we actually had to mow the grass and pull weeds. Friday was the day we cleaned the bays, and I enjoyed that. We took everything out of the bay, reorganized the bunker gear and medical equipment, and sprayed, scrubbed, and squeegeed the floors.

Saturdays were easier, as most were spent training with people who were going to paramedic school and had to put in their hours riding with departments. That was fun when I worked busy stations, because trainees were enthusiastic and talented when it came to medical procedures such as IVs, intubation, and various types of trauma response. The extra pairs of hands were great to have on calls—especially for the rescues that only had two para-medics on duty.

The only so-called rest day was Sunday, which just meant there weren't chores to do when we weren't out on calls. And it was a good thing, too, because Sundays could turn out to be very busy shifts, especially if you worked areas that covered the major highways like

Alligator Alley, the east and west route from Fort Lauderdale to Naples. We also covered I-95, the turnpike, I-595, and the Sawgrass Expressway, where folks drove like they were on the speedway. I didn't mind working that day because the white shirts and the brass from downtown were off. When I was an officer, my rule for the crews was to check out the trucks and equipment, go to the grocery store early, and then just run the calls. I never wanted to be a ballbuster and insist on training that day. Some officers did, and it sucked. They would plan multi-company drills on Sundays, and I believed it hurt morale. We busted our asses all week, and the crew had more than earned a day to watch sports between calls.

SIX

EVERYONE DESERVES SAVING

There was another fire station further south, just across Highway 441 from the Seminole Reservation. It was just as busy, and the area was diverse, too, with a large Native American population and plenty of commercial property. We ran lots of fires in the area, particularly in one dicey old trailer park west of town called Silver Oaks. There was trash everywhere, and the indoor living conditions were horrific. In contrast, there was a different trailer park in the same area, but it was filled with senior citizens, and for the most part, it was spotless. Those elderly people took pride in what little they had, and I could relate to that, having grown up in modest conditions myself.

My childhood home was a small, immaculate house with gray wallpaper printed with big pink roses. The floor was linoleum, and a bread box sat on the metal countertop in our tiny kitchen. A curtain off to the side of the kitchen hid the pot, which we all used in the absence of an inside bathroom. This primitive setup was an embarrassment when I was a little girl, and it made it impossible for me to ask friends to come over and play. But my mother took pride in our home, and she taught me to do the same.

"We are poor," she would say, "but we are not pigs, and a bar of soap doesn't cost that much." Our house was spotless, and you could eat off the worn linoleum floor. Growing up in my mother's house, the first order of the day was to make my bed, and I still do that today. I cannot stand going to bed with messed-up sheets, so each morning I shake everything out and do hospital corners. You could bounce a quarter off the bed after I make it; that was a rule I enforced in the firehouse, too.

When I ran calls in expensive neighborhoods where clothes were piled to the ceiling and dirty dishes filled the sink—this nastiness from people who had more than I could ever have dreamed of having grown up as a poor kid—I would reflect back to my childhood and how clean and neat my little home was kept. I also remember running calls in poor neighborhoods that were kept as clean and neat as mine had been years ago.

What I learned from all this is that money has nothing to do with self-respect or class. Throughout the years of running calls on people living in mansions, trailers, storage sheds, tents, alleys behind businesses, and encampments in the woods, I tried to approach every person on every call the same way: with caution and respect, and to always have an exit strategy for the crews involved just in case things turned crazy.

Anyway, the captain of this station near Silver Oaks was an old-timer from Hackensack, New Jersey. The rumor was that he didn't like women in the fire service, because he didn't think they could do the job. I didn't let it faze me. This captain took particular pride in flushing fire hydrants, and he would bring the caps back to the station to clean and paint them before returning them to their rightful places on the hydrants. He wouldn't talk to you if he didn't like you, and I was smart enough to never ask him why. I kept my mouth shut, checked all the engine equipment thoroughly, and did everything that needed to be done around the station without ever having to be asked. In other words, I stayed out of his way and kept busy.

Sure enough, when nighttime came and the tones went off—"Structure Fire, multiple reports, Silver Oaks Trailer Park"—the captain shouted to me, "Probie, let's go!"

"Yes, sir," I responded, my heart pounding as I ran out to the bay, kicking off my shoes, jumping into my bunker pants and boots, tightening my red suspenders, throwing on my Nomex hood and bunker coat, and climbing up into the jump seat open cab sitting backward as the driver looked back at me, before giving him the thumbs-up sign to take off. The engine pulled quickly out onto the street, lights and sirens blasting as I scrambled to get my seatbelt buckled so I wouldn't fall out as the driver hauled ass to the scene. We wanted to beat any other engine that might be responding with us to the fire.

These trailer park fires could get out of hand fast, and we hoped the volunteers would show up to help. There weren't too many other engine companies responding to calls with us in those days, and you dared not call for mutual aid either. Most of the other departments hated us, and we them, so usually, if they showed up on our scene, the chief would cancel them upon arrival. Yes, our department was still the red-headed stepchild, but we were tough and didn't take shit from anybody. We busted our asses and were proud of our aggressive tactics. Our motto was, "Put the wet stuff on the red stuff, and just put the damn thing out. Everyone goes home safe in the morning." Still, it would have been nice to have some extra help, because three people on an engine aren't nearly enough.

The captain turned around in his seat, banging on the window that separated us and yelling, "Smoke showing! Get ready!" I turned and glanced out of the front windshield of the engine, and yes, there it was: hell. A huge column of black smoke swirled in the night air, and we were heading straight for it. I was excited, my adrenaline pumping as I methodically put on my fire gloves, turned on the bottle of my air pack, and got my mask ready to put on upon arrival. I was also trying to get my thoughts together and remember all of my training and experience, concentrating on what I had to do when the engine stopped at the hydrant in the park, close to the fire.

"Get off and wrap the hydrant, then hurry and get back on the truck, probie," the captain yelled, and I did just that, not paying any attention to the curious bystanders that seem to show up whenever there's an emergency. I jumped back onto the truck, and we pulled up to a well-involved single-wide trailer. I grabbed a one-and-a-half-inch hose line from the truck, pulled the line to the front door of the trailer, bled the air out of the charged line, and put my mask on, tightening the straps. Then I pulled my Nomex hood over my head for safety before fastening my helmet. I felt the door before opening it carefully, always kneeling at the side of the opening in case of a backdraft. Opening a door like this is dangerous because if all of the windows are shut and the contents inside come to their ignition temperature, introducing oxygen without ventilation first can kill you. Safe, I entered the trailer, opening the line and changing the nozzle pattern as needed with the captain right behind me giving me instructions and keeping the hose line from getting kinked. What a rush!

When the flames had subsided, he called "fire out" on the radio to dispatch. We performed salvage and overhaul, protecting items that weren't damaged and checking every room, nook, and cranny for possible fire extension. It's an amateur mistake to have to return to a rekindle of a fire you've just put out. Then we proceeded to drain the dirty hose and roll fifty-foot sections into donuts, which we stacked on the tailboard of the truck, along with any tools and equipment we'd used, to clean back at the station. Then the fun part: draining and repacking the large-diameter hose, which was four inches at that time and connected to the hydrant supplying water to the pump of the engine. Since the engine's tank held 500 to 750 gallons, it was imperative to have an ongoing supply of water. The worst thing you could do is run out of water on a fire.

Thank goodness I wasn't doing all this alone. I enjoyed listening to the old-timer's stories about working by themselves before I was hired, but I could never imagine driving the engine to a fire, putting it in pump mode, grabbing the hose, fighting a fire alone, then salvage and overhaul to make sure the fire was out, then repacking the hose—doing all of that on my own before driving back to the station to get ready for the next call. They were happy to see volunteers or maybe another guy responding from a station close by. And again, that person was all by himself. Talk about tough. Those guys were my inspiration for sure.

This wasn't the only fire we put out at Silver Oaks, nor was it the most difficult. When they're on fire, single-wide trailers can be reduced to shells in approximately seven minutes, and they're dangerous as hell. But hey, every trailer was somebody's home, so we gave it our all, just like we would for any other structure fire. There was a small department located near Silver Oaks that had standing orders not to go inside and fight fires there offensively. Rather, they were only to perform outside defensive tactics and let the structures themselves burn. One time, they arrived to a Silver Oaks call before my engine company. When we arrived, I jumped off the truck ready to go and saw them all standing outside, doing the huddle while the trailer continued to burn. I grabbed the charged hose line out of the firefighter's hand and said, "Give me that hose, you pussy." Then I proceeded to enter the burning trailer and put the fire out.

It was quite the talk of the department for years to come, and one of my favorite guys in the department even broadcasted the story to every station in the department years later, reminiscing with the other guys on the truck without realizing his dispatch mic was open. Nobody from the upper echelon got in trouble for my "insubordination," fortunately. And those guys who'd doubted I could do the job? After that fire, they all knew I would get in there and get down and dirty to do what needed to be done.

Meanwhile, back at the station, exhausted, we washed the filthy fire hose with soap and water and snaked it into an S-formation out on the concrete ramp to dry. Then we washed the air packs, changed the bottles, and repacked the cross lays with clean, dry hose before washing tools and any other equipment as fast as we could to get it back into service and ready for the next run.

When we finished and I went inside the station to wash up, the captain said to me, "Good job, probie." Little did I know at the time how golden those words were. I found out later that he'd called my training officer and told him, "That split tail can work with me anytime." Choice language aside, that was as big a compliment as you could get from the crusty, old captain. I worked with him many times after that, and we always got along just fine. Once our shift was over, he would put on his Hawaiian shirt and his big straw hat. The funny thing was, he couldn't stand the other woman who got hired with me. He never spoke a word to her and didn't want her on his truck, even though she was a kickass firefighter, too.

I was young, gutsy, and fearless. There was something so empowering to me about being a firefighter. I felt like I had a shield of armor at times, and I knew I was genuinely meant to help anyone in need, whether they lived in a squalid trailer park or a splendid mansion. Although I was well aware of the danger, I was ready and willing to meet the challenge.

SEVEN

PROVING MYSELF: TO MY CREW AND MYSELF

It was great to be out into the field, continuing my training through work at different stations. My favorite was located by the infamous Swap Shop, an enormous drive-in theater that doubles as a flea market. This was a busy station, to say the least. In the early 1990s, it was listed in *Firehouse Magazine* as the ninth busiest engine company in the nation. You could get a structure fire or two, multiple kinds of trauma, and everything from car accidents to shootings and stabbings out of that station—sometimes all in one shift. In fact, it wasn't unusual to run twenty-five to thirty calls in a twenty-four-hour shift, and that was on the engine alone. The station housed a rescue truck, too, though since there were only two paramedics on it, the engine would respond with them to assist in any way needed.

There were multiple gangs operating in the area, and they were all trying to eliminate each other to claim their turf. The preferred method was to shoot their target in the femoral artery so they would bleed out quickly. Needless to say, this kept our rescue crew busy. To save our patients, we had to cut off all their clothes to see just what we were working with and to give us an opportunity to stop the bleeding. On one of those calls, as I prepared to cut off the victim's pants to reveal all that his maker had given him, the guys working with me chanted, "Oh, my God, I can't believe my eyes, Schooner!" They tried their best to embarrass me, but I just kept on cutting. By that point, looking at naked men with bullet holes in them seemed like no big deal to me. My job was to do the best I could within the scope of my training to stop the bleeding, stabilize the patient, and assist the paramedics in packaging them for transport to a trauma center. Sometimes they lived, and sometimes, despite our best efforts, they died.

We responded to an unknown medical call on the engine, and upon arrival, we found the victim lying in the middle of the field with a flathead axe embedded in the top of his skull. His eyes were open, but his pupils were fixed and staring straight ahead. I was only an EMT at the time, so my training was limited to taking his vitals, attaching a nasal cannula to give him oxygen, stabilizing him on a backboard, and applying a cervical collar to keep his neck in alignment. I was careful not to remove the embedded axe, because that could lead to uncontrollable bleeding that would all but eliminate the patient's chance of survival. Instead, I secured it in place while I waited for the paramedics to arrive for transport, all the while keeping my eyes and ears open in case the attacker decided to come back and finish the job.

"Nope, we didn't see nothin'," said the people we asked for information about what had happened. I found this to be just a little sketchy and odd since it was broad daylight, in a field and just yards from the local convenience store in the hood. There was always a large crowd of people going in and out to buy beer, cigarettes, milk, diapers, and, if we're being honest, probably some illegal substances, too. Surely, someone had seen something. But in this part of town, saying something meant you could end up suffering the same fate or worse.

Some of our rescue calls came directly from law enforcement as well, after undercover officers would conduct raids in the neighborhood. These usually happened on Friday nights, and I remember one in particular when we were called to check out a patient they had arrested. He was a White male wearing a white shirt, a striped tie, and black slacks. He'd probably just gotten off work nearby, in downtown Fort Lauderdale. He had been buying dime bags of crack cocaine and, upon getting caught, he'd decided to swallow them all. As an EMT, I took his vital signs, administered oxygen, and gathered medical history, including the approximate amount of crack he'd ingested, so I could relay it all to the paramedics once they arrived. This guy was a puddle of anxious sweat, and all I could think of was how much trouble he'd be in if he even survived this stupid act of desperation.

Unfortunately, these weren't my first experiences with patients who weren't likely to make it. I did my required ride time for EMT with a department north of Broward County. The requirements were to show up on time—early if you were smart and wanted to make a good impression—wear a watch with a second hand, carry a stethoscope, and look professional, wearing neatly pressed clothing and the smock bearing the name of your school. The paramedic who had agreed to be your preceptor was in charge, and they could send your ass home if they weren't impressed with your thirst for learning or your ability to show up on time. They could call the school and get you kicked out of the program if you didn't follow the rules.

Along with these explicit rules, there were also unofficial rules for EMT trainees to follow when they were in the firehouse. Those of us, like me, who were also cutting our teeth as new firefighters, knew and obeyed them without question. But the students who weren't already firefighters didn't know what it took to do the job, and they took a lot of grief when they couldn't even follow these basic guidelines:

1. No sitting in the recliners.

2. No sitting in the chairs facing the TV when at the kitchen table.

3. No falling asleep.

4. Keep your study material out of the way of the on-duty crews.

5. Introduce yourself respectfully, and don't speak unless spoken to.

6. Bring money for lunch and dinner so if they like you and want to include you, you'll be able to pay your own way. And if you are included, be the first one to start cleaning up the kitchen after the meal.

7. Be a sponge and absorb all the training and information that you can.

One of the first calls I responded to as an EMT student was a horrific car wreck on I-95 in Delray Beach. It was nasty. The girl was young and had been driving drunk with her dog in the back seat. Beer cans covered the floorboards. We transported her to the trauma center, hoping to save her life. The surgical crew asked us if we wanted to witness them cracking her chest in an attempt to resuscitate her. Of course, we said yes, so they cracked her chest and massaged her heart while I was there with her. I will never forget holding her hand

before the procedure, while she kept telling me, "I am so cold."
What an experience. She died, and while it was routine, on-the-job
training for me, the finality and fragility of life took my breath away.
That was my first experience with trauma and death, but it certainly
wouldn't be my last.

Sometimes, calls that originally came in as "unknown medical" would evolve into something entirely different by the time
we arrived on scene. There was always a chance that the situation
would turn out to be dangerous, so it was imperative to ask dispatch
for updates on police activity, potential criminal activity, and the
patient's mental status. It wasn't uncommon for us to stage a block
away until the police could arrive and secure the scene for our safety.
Of course, we had officers who thought they were bulletproof and
refused to wait, but when they'd knock on the door only to find
themselves looking down the barrel of a gun, they'd learn their
lesson the scary way.

As these traumatic experiences became more and more commonplace, I realized that having the right crew around you could be the
difference between thriving and not. Firefighters are a clannish
bunch, and you are either in or out. I learned quickly that when
the crew teased you, that was a good sign. It meant they liked and
trusted you. If they shunned you, either on the scene of a call or
back at the station, it was a bad sign. One officer, one of my favorite
lieutenants, was the ultimate trickster, and he loved to play the same
joke on every newbie.

We performed fire hydrant maintenance in our district to ensure
they were all functioning properly and ready when we needed them.
Each hydrant had three caps—two small ones and a large steamer
cap. We would start by taking them all off and greasing them if
needed, then we'd put the two smallest caps back on. With the large

steamer cap still off, we'd open the hydrant up all the way, letting it run until the water flowed clear. Sometimes the residents would come outside and talk to us while we did this, so it was good PR for the department, too.

Well, the first time I participated in hydrant maintenance, this lieutenant and I pulled up to one particular hydrant in someone's front yard, and he told me to go ahead and flush it. Well, it took me a minute to realize after struggling to remove the caps that this fire hydrant was actually a yard decoration. The woman who lived in the house was a firefighter who worked at another department, and of course, she was in on the joke. She would come out, laughing, and say, "Are you doing this again to this poor probie?" The lieutenant would grin and, more often than not, the probie would laugh with him. I certainly did. This man didn't have a mean bone in his body.

The captain in charge of another station, on the other hand, took a different approach. Upon arriving at the hydrant to be serviced, he would set his stopwatch and yell, "Run!" I'd jump off the truck, hydrant wrench in one hand and a bottle of grease in the other, and off I would go. Some caps were on so damn tight I had to use the wrench to break them free. Then I'd spin them off, grease them, put the two small caps back on, and open the hydrant all the way to flush the crappy orange rust water out until it was clear. Then I'd close the hydrant, put the steamer cap back on, run back to the engine, step up into the jump seat, and away we would go, on to the next one, and repeat.

I'd work with purpose, but I was never focused on beating the stopwatch. It was tedious, but if he thought he was going to break me with that silly bullshit, he had to think again. One of the guys who got hired with me didn't fare as well. After doing twenty-five to thirty hydrants by himself in the Florida summer sun, under the pressure of the captain's timer, he got sick, probably from heat exhaustion, and had to go home.

Character matters, and this officer was questionable. I like Maya Angelou's phrase, "The first time someone shows you who they are, believe them." There were officers who led by example and others who used their rank and authority to intimidate those below them. As I gained more experience, I knew that I wanted to be an officer, and I decided to get my associate's degree in fire science (the pinnacle of education when I started). But the degree didn't teach me what kind of officer I wanted to be—it took these kinds of job experiences to learn that. I had worked with and observed many different kinds of leaders already and would continue to do so throughout my career. I always tried to emulate the "good ones," working to build the character traits I admired in the officers I respected greatly. Working with officers who were harder to respect just cemented my goal of becoming one myself, and I vowed never to disrespect the men and women under my command.

But I still had a way to go before reaching that goal. When I passed my final evaluations and my probationary year was over, it was such a moment of relief. Now I was officially a "rookie." I relaxed a little, but not much.

I would sometimes wonder how all this had happened. How did this little girl from Portage, Ohio, where expectations were low, to say the least, make it as a firefighter? Too many of the people I grew up with in that depressed little hometown ended up in prison, hooked on different distractions, or dead.

How did I break that cycle? I chose to bust my ass, requesting placement at the busiest stations to gain experience while working toward my degree in fire science. Earning that associate's degree would lead to a pay increase, but more importantly, it would allow me to start taking promotional exams for both driver-engineer and fire lieutenant. My department was bare bones when it came to promotions, but it did upgrade me in both positions for years after I passed the written and practical exams. Passing the tests didn't guarantee me a promotion—rather, they classified me as an "upgrade" and put me on the list to be promoted when an opportunity became available. I sucked at taking tests, and in those days, if you weren't number one or two on the list, there was no promotion, and you'd have to test once again when the list expired. So it was a slow process. I became an upgrade driver and an upgrade fire lieutenant, taking the test every two years for approximately twelve years until I earned my promotions. During that time, I drove fire engines, ladder trucks, tanker trucks, and once I became a paramedic in 2001, rescue trucks, too. I might have grumbled sometimes, but I wasn't about to give up until I got promoted.

EIGHT

FAMILY TIES: BY BLOOD AND BY FIRE

The discipline, thoroughness, and cleanliness of the firehouse doctrine spoke to me. I had a thing for keeping files and paperwork in order, too, likely thanks to my background in banking and office work. As an officer, whenever I had the time, I would assign one of the probies to assist me in cleaning out ancient paperwork. Although I kept files on the station computer, it always made sense to me to keep hard copies as backup. I would take pride in keeping my office organized, with up-to-date manuals and clipboards displaying orders and daily checkout instructions. I wanted everything in its place and easy to see. Messiness just compounds laziness, in my opinion, and that goes for keeping the trucks and stations clean, too. Not to mention my crews. I have been known to iron a guy's shirt if it wasn't looking neat enough. It pained me to see somebody with a wrinkled shirt or pants, especially when we had to go out in public. Again, people take notice whenever they see us getting off a fire or rescue truck, and we owe it to them and our department to look professional.

I come by it naturally, though. My mom used to iron my dad's white concrete pants and even his plain white T-shirts. She'd lay those pants out on the ironing board, staple the cuffs, spray them with Niagara Falls starch, and iron them until they were flawless, all with the radio on in the background. My mother, being from Kentucky, loved country music, so we'd listen to Loretta Lynn, Dolly Parton, Porter Wagoner, The Skaggs Brothers, and of course, Willie Nelson (and this was back when he had short hair and was clean-shaven).

My father loved music, too. He would whistle tunes in perfect key as he walked down the sidewalk. If I misbehaved, he would tell me to "straighten up and fly right," and I didn't know until years later that that line was from a famous old song. My parents were big into the old-time entertainment shows, and *Hee-Haw*, *Austin City Limits*, and the like were often our entertainment on Friday and Saturday nights.

Anyway, Mom saw wrinkled clothes as a sign of sloppiness or laziness, and I inherited her habit. Even now that I'm retired, I love to iron, and I use copious amounts of spray starch. I find it relaxing, and there is something satisfying about the precision of the job. When I'm ironing clothes and listening to music, I feel close to my mom, too.

While I can explain the affinity for ironing, it was interesting that I liked the rest of the military-style life, given some of my early exposure to it. My brother got drafted into the Army when he was only eighteen years old and was sent to boot camp in the Carolinas. He was a gentle giant at six-foot-eight, and he always stood up for the little guys who were bullied. I never found out the whole story, since I was a kid at the time, but supposedly he was constantly threatened in the Army and decided he would rather ditch boot camp and come home alive. In other words, he went AWOL. Multiple times. He got picked up and returned to boot camp three times, but the fourth was the charm.

When it happened, I was riding with him in his 1957 Chevy, the two of us following our parents to Florida, where Dad would work as a brick mason for the summer and we would visit my sister and brother-in-law, who were living in Cocoa. We had the radio blasting as always, playing '60s and early '70s rock and roll, singing to our hearts' content, when *bam!*

It was quite a shock to me, an eleven—almost twelve—year-old girl, when suddenly a car pulled up next to us with the window down, flashing a badge and yelling, "FBI, pull over!"

We did.

One of the agents opened the driver's side car door, yanked my brother out from behind the wheel, handcuffed him, and threw him into the back of their unmarked car. His partner took my brother's place in the driver's seat and started the engine. I was totally distraught by this point, screaming and crying, and yelling, "No! Where are you taking my brother?"

The agent just looked over at me, saying, "He'll be fine," and then drove the Chevy off to catch up with my parents. After he handed me off to them, we continued our drive to Florida, shocked and saddened. My brother ended up spending a couple of years in Leavenworth prison, and then he lived with some of my parents' friends in Ohio after he was dishonorably discharged from the Army. I don't know why he didn't come to Florida after he got out, but I didn't see him for over two years, and that terrible incident ruined his life. The only thing he would tell me when I grew up was that he wasn't scared of going to Vietnam, but he figured he would be killed in boot camp before he ever got the chance.

I have great respect and admiration for men and women who join the military, though it was never a consideration for me, especially after my brother's experience. My brother-in-law was a career Navy man, and he retired as a master chief of recruiting in the Northeast.

His ceremony was held on the *USS Constitution*, and he had four admirals in attendance. My father told us later that our family had been investigated before my brother-in-law married my oldest sister. I don't know exactly what that entailed, but I do know he traveled the world and handled some precarious situations in dicey places. He was pretty shocked when my sister brought him home to our house and he saw firsthand just how poor we were. He and my oldest sister would take me back to Norfolk in the summertime to stay with them. I loved seeing my brother-in-law and visiting the Navy base, seeing all of the men and women in their crisp white uniforms. Maybe that had a subconscious impression on me that led me to commit myself to the fire service.

• • •

I was the youngest child in my family, and there were sixteen years between me and my oldest sister. My next sister was five years younger than my oldest, and my brother came five years after that. Six and a half years later, I arrived. I became an aunt when I was only nine years old, and both of my sisters were married and living in other parts of the country, so I really felt like an only child sometimes. My brother and I were close, and he acted like my protector, but he also didn't hesitate to drag my ass home if he found me hanging out with unscrupulous people or potentially getting into trouble. But because he was so much older, we certainly didn't hang out together. The fire service—where I'd get to live twenty-four or more hours with people, all of us working and cooking meals together—fulfilled my desire for that close family unit I had missed growing up.

Unlike blood family, the firehouse family is connected by experiences—good, bad, horrific, tragic, funny, and everything in between—along with camaraderie and time on the job. And if you're lucky, you keep that family strong by maintaining contact with a few special souls after retirement. Don't get me wrong, there is plenty of conflict—sometimes quite heated—on issues as mundane as how much coffee to make to as serious as how to approach a difficult IV or intubation on a particular patient. You might argue over who grabbed the nozzle first and proceeded to kick a fire's ass or over who captured the most attention from the opposite sex in the grocery store.

Beyond the conflict and ribbing, though, there's deep loyalty, as we firefighters understand each other's experiences in a way few outsiders can. So we look after each other. We recognize each other's coping mechanisms, and we strive to support one another the best we can.

One of the old-time chiefs on my shift was quite a funny guy. He couldn't say my name correctly, so he always called me Sidney. He really had a good heart, and he was a smart guy when he was sober, but he also had an alcohol problem. He would be out of the station all day doing whatever chiefs did, and then he would stumble back around dinnertime with Chinese food and a carton of chocolate milk. We'd look after him, and he'd eat his dinner and go to bed.

We figured this chief was dealing with personal issues, and the firehouse was his refuge. We were his family, so we didn't judge him. And besides, he was a fair man—a good chief who listened when you screwed up and didn't just push you out the door to be fired like some other chiefs might have done.

I know his drinking on the job wouldn't fly today, and I certainly don't condone the behavior, but like I said, the firehouse was a very different place in the late 1980s, and there was a lot we let slide that we wouldn't now. I realize how potentially harmful some of those behaviors were, but our fire family maintained a sense of compassion and duty, and we took care of our own. We were also referred to counseling and treatment if needed, rather than sent packing. I am not going to be all "Pollyanna" about it, but supporting rather than condemning one another when we happened to be in a mess saved a lot of good people's careers.

We firefighters are a very empathetic bunch, and if we can't help our own, then what does that say about us? One of our chiefs who started with FDNY back in the day said they were allotted one beer after a structure fire. Our department didn't have that policy, but after a hot, physically exhausting fire, it sure sounded refreshing to me.

The point is, your fire rescue family is sacred, despite the snoring, farting, and regularly scheduled juvenile behavior in the bunkroom at night. And over breakfast or dinner you get to hear all of the complaints and the gossip: who hates who, who is getting divorced, who has a girlfriend on the side, and who is dealing with their kids' problems—from bratty behavior or bad grades to drugs or worse. You know who in your family is suddenly dealing with medical issues, whether their own or their parents' or spouses', and you know who's grieving the loss of a loved one. And all these problems become all of ours to try to solve as we sit at the fire family table. This is when we talk, tease, cry, and console each other—whatever is needed for any given situation on any given day.

That's just life in a family.

Time passes, and people retire or leave assignments. Sometimes tragedy strikes or illness takes someone from us. I never want to candy coat the profession, but my firefighting family is the best family that I have ever known.

NINE

FREEDOM AND ROMANCE

Now that I had a real profession, with a good paycheck and benefits, my former longtime boyfriend had begged me to take him back and try again. I agreed and moved back into our old apartment with him, but it wasn't destined to last. While I will now say, many years later, that he was a good guy and I could have done a lot worse, the reality is that he wasn't the man for me. I was seventeen when we'd started dating, and I was young, insecure, and impressionable. But at age thirty-one, I had matured, found my confidence and voice, and sought to find my own way in life. I didn't need or want to be dependent on a man for my happiness or financial security.

And besides, somebody much better for me was on the horizon, and his green eyes had already caught mine.

Remember the man I met on my first day as a probie? The one delivering telephone poles for the recruits to chop? And remember the man I had to share a room with, who drove me nuts by insisting on sleeping in only his briefs? The one I told you would become much more important later on? Well, here's a secret: Those two men were one and the same: my future husband, Mark. He was single, gorgeous, and kept me on my toes. It was instantaneous combustion the moment I laid eyes on him, but it took us a little while to get together. He still teases me to this day with a funny interpretation of one of our early flirtations. He says I pushed him up against the chief's car one morning and said, "You have the most incredible green eyes that I have ever seen." Well, I didn't push him up against anything, but one morning before getting off duty, I looked at him, smitten, and said, "You have beautiful green eyes." He would turn out to be the one, and he romanced me like I had never dreamed possible. I was thirty-one, and he was twenty-seven; both of us had lived and loved others, and frankly, I just thought romance was something I read about in a book or saw in the movies. I was wrong.

Fast forward about a month from that flirtatious morning. I had just finished EMT school and was preparing to take the state test, but it was in Miami, and I didn't know exactly where the test site was located. (This was prior to GPS.) Well, it just so happened that the object of my desire had lived in Miami while he was in the Coast Guard, and he offered to drive me there to take the test. I didn't object.

Afterward, it was late and getting dark, so we stopped to have dinner at a local steak house. It was wonderful, and so was the company. He then dropped me off at my apartment with nothing but a simple, "Goodnight. See you on shift." He was a complete gentleman, and the wheels of fate started turning that night.

After I found out that I'd passed my EMT test and was now state-certified, I decided to make sure he knew that, on my next Kelly day, I planned to drive down to the keys to celebrate by relaxing in the sun. My boyfriend, with whom things were already feeling stagnant, was visiting his parents in Long Island, and I was long overdue for a break. I swear, I heard George Michael singing in my ear: "Freedom!"

It was amazing how good it felt to be alone, driving to the keys in that open Jeep, smelling the salt air and admiring the beautiful turquoise water on both sides of the road. It was mesmerizing. I'd booked a room in a cute little hotel called The Sands for the weekend, and I reveled in the fact that I could now afford to go to a nice restaurant and treat myself to a decent meal. After testing for a year, I was officially a paid professional firefighter, and I would get a pay raise now that I'd passed my EMT classes, too. This set of circumstances would prove to be my first lottery ticket in life.

Growing up in Cocoa after my sister and brother-in-law became my legal guardians at the age of thirteen cemented my love of the sand, surf, and ocean—largely because I spent more of my days hitchhiking to Cocoa Beach than going to school. Back then, I was young, skinny, and golden from the sun. Girls like me were called "Cocoa Beach Cuties," Ron Jon's was just a small surf shack on A1A, and you could watch the space shuttles blast off from the jetty park in Cape Canaveral. The launchpad was about ten miles north, directly across the inlet.

In those days, it was natural for me to be lying on the beach in a tiny string bikini, and that's exactly what I was doing in the keys all those years later: soaking up the sun, eyes closed, stretched out on a beach recliner, listening to music on my portable radio.

The sun and the stars must have been aligned perfectly that day, because after not too long, I heard a voice say, "Hello there." Opening my eyes, I saw him standing there in the sand at the foot of my recliner, fishing pole in hand. He was wearing a million-dollar smile and Ray-Bans that hid those beautiful green eyes. He was tan, sleek, and lean as a cat.

"I decided to come down here and do some fishing," he said, "so I thought I would look you up."

We had dinner that night, including a copious amount of wine, and the wheels of lust and longing joined the wheels of fate. There was no turning back now. It would be strange to pretend we were just coworkers when on duty at the station. There was no way we could keep our secret for long, and now I had some important decisions to make.

Those decisions turned out to be some of the easiest I'd ever made.

By the time my boyfriend returned from visiting his parents, I had already found an efficiency apartment on the beach above a hair salon, paid the rent, and I was ecstatic. I left our shared apartment without taking so much as a towel. Nothing except my cat Bogey. I needed a new start and didn't want any reminders of my old life. I had never been able to qualify for a credit card, but now that I had a good steady job, I got one at 24-percent interest. The first thing I purchased was a bed, and then I got to work painting my apartment exactly the color I wanted: peach. This was the first time I'd really been out on my own since I was sixteen years old, and it felt damn good.

Although I was falling for my green-eyed man quickly, I kept it in check, knowing that I would never live long-term with any man again unless he put a ring on it, and I was in no hurry.

On my own, living on the beach in my peach-colored studio with my cat was a dream come true. I absolutely loved my new career and budding romance, and life was good. After all the years I had just managed to squeak by financially, working meaningless jobs for a steady paycheck, this new beginning was a dream to me. I cannot emphasize enough how important it is for a woman to have her own financial power and to control her own destiny. Some never get the chance, and that is a shame. Becoming a firefighter and knowing I would be scrutinized by both men and women, I wanted to set a good example and show young girls anything was possible. I wanted to be a living reminder that, if you work hard, take your own reins, and prioritize your independence, you can achieve anything—even and especially success in predominantly male professions.

Yes, my personal life was on a positive roll. After my green-eyed man and I had been dating for approximately one year, he started insisting that we move in together. He and another firefighter were living in a rented house across town, and it could take almost an hour for him to drive to my apartment on the beach.

I had sworn to myself that I'd never live with another man unless he was my husband, so I had to think long and hard about that. We were spending a lot of time together at that point, and he was incredibly romantic. He would visit my little apartment and bring bags of groceries, dishes, pots and pans, and even plants to spruce the place up. I was floating around to different stations by that time, and he got teased constantly by the guys at work for sending balloons to wherever I was working. I was wooed, courted, wined, and dined, and I loved it. I loved him. But I still felt I needed to keep my wits about me so I wouldn't get my heart broken again. Fortunately, having financial independence, job satisfaction, and a few more years under my belt allowed me to keep my head from spinning. Still, despite all my rationality, the cat was definitely out of the bag, and we could no longer work together.

Right before Thanksgiving that year, he told me he was flying to California to spend the holiday with his parents. I was bummed we wouldn't be able to spend that time together, but I understood. They had rented a house on the northern coast in scenic Mendocino, looking out over the beautiful Pacific Ocean.

He and his twin sister were born near San Diego, and his whole family had lived in Berkeley while their father got his doctorate in entomology. I had only dreamed of ever seeing California, but he had loved it there. When his dad got a job as a research scientist for the University of Tallahassee, he said it felt as though his world was crashing in. He was only fourteen, and it was a brutal awakening. I say he went from heaven to hell while I went from hell to heaven, because Florida compared to Berkeley may have seemed like hell, but compared to Ohio, it was heaven.

Shortly after he told me about the trip, I arrived home after shift to find a bag of groceries and a small plant sitting on my kitchen counter. Imagine how shocked I was when, inside the paper grocery bag, I found a round-trip ticket to San Francisco in my name! Oh, my god. He'd also bought me a beautiful cream-colored jumpsuit with a brown braided belt and a pair of Italian boots from my favorite store: Banana Republic. He told me he wanted me to fly out there during his visit. He would pick me up at the airport, and we would drive along the coast to Mendocino, where he wanted me to meet his parents. He was determined and in love, and so was I. The California trip sealed it for me.

How could I not be hopelessly in love after spending the holiday meeting his parents (whom I loved despite my fears that they would intimidate me with their cerebral brilliance), seeing the coast, and luxuriating in the hot tub behind this gorgeous house on the cliffs overlooking the ocean? But needless to say, they welcomed me warmly, and my fears of not being accepted disappeared. (To be honest, I think I won his parents over with my quirky fashion sense. I wore a tie-dyed T-shirt tied up in the front, a skirt made from a pair of blue jeans with white fabric billowing out below the knee, and my favorite pink Converse high-tops. I was a redhead at that time, and I sported a red bandana tied up like a headband.)

Once we returned to Florida, I cautiously agreed that we should move in together, somewhere completely new and larger than my studio apartment. I also had a relatively short timeline in my mind for living together before making things official. We moved first to a brand-new apartment west of town, but I was like a fish out of water living so far away from the ocean. So we packed up again and moved to a tiny one-bedroom studio close to the beach, trading in the space for the downtown living I craved.

After we'd lived together for about a year, he asked me to accompany him on a trip to Tallahassee so I could meet his high school buddy who also happened to be from California. I had never visited this part of Florida, and it was all very different from the East Coast. I was enchanted by its lovely old oak trees and hills.

During that trip, he took me to MacClay Gardens, a state park full of beautiful flowers. I stopped to admire a particular bloom, and when I turned back to look at him, he reached beneath the flower, pulled out a blue box, kneeled, and proposed to me in the most proper way. Of course, I said yes, and one year later, in 1990, we flew to Jamaica, just the two of us, to be married on the beach at sunset. I wore a long, ivory-colored lace gown that cost me three hundred dollars—a lot of money when I was only making nine bucks an hour—and he was so handsome in a white tuxedo with a turquoise cummerbund. A Jamaican preacher married us, and the only attendants were our witnesses, who worked at the resort. Upon our return, we had a killer party at a local park with all of our firefighter friends, complete with a cake decorated with drawings of a male and female firefighter dancing in their bunker gear and helmets.

Then it was back to work for both of us. We didn't work together once we became a couple and definitely not once we got married. We worked on the same shifts (at different stations) for fifteen years so we could enjoy our off days together. After that, we got a dog, and so we decided to go on different shifts.

I knew of married couples who were paramedics and worked on the same rescue truck. I could never imagine doing that. Working a twenty-four-hour shift with your significant other and then going home together would be too much togetherness for me. Fortunately, my new husband felt the same way.

When we did find ourselves on the same call, we remained consummate professionals, never hugging or kissing each other in the station, and certainly not in public or on an emergency call. The public didn't know we were married, since wedding bands were a safety hazard in our industry. The last thing we wanted to happen was for one of us to suffer a degloving injury. We were confident in our marriage, and we trusted each other, so not wearing a ring wasn't a problem. He is very handsome, though, and he had a number of admirers. It was funny to see them try to cozy up to him on a scene. He wasn't interested, and I was secure in our relationship. Besides, I was adamant about not showing any affection to my husband if we happened to be on the same incident, because it would feed into the dialogue that men and women shouldn't work together, particularly as firefighters.

• • •

Once I married the bright light of my life, on February 23rd, 1990, we decided to move out of Broward County, where we worked, for a number of reasons. For one, it was exhausting to see fire trucks with familiar faces on them and wonder what catastrophe our friends and colleagues were facing every time we heard a siren. We also both felt it was important to develop friendships with people who weren't in the business, as well. Firefighters and paramedics can be very clannish, and their conversations almost always revolve around work. Only those of us in the business understand our demented sense of humor. That is fine, and I cherish those bonds, but there are plenty of interesting people who do other things for a living, and we wanted to meet them, too.

Another big factor was that houses were a lot cheaper farther away from Fort Lauderdale. Both of us liked being close to the beach, but that real estate was out of our price range back then. We wanted a house, a yard, and most of all, a German shepherd. So, we found an old-style Florida ranch house with a huge backyard.

It was a money pit.

Most notably, the house was in a flood zone, and it flooded three times in the twelve years we lived there. Eventually, we sold it and moved into a tiny one-bedroom, one-bath apartment, where we stayed until we were able to build a new house in a beautiful new neighborhood located on a preserve further north of our money pit in Martin County. It was lovely, and it was low-maintenance. We went through four major hurricanes in 2004, and we never sprung a leak. We'd lost our beloved first German shepherd, Indy, to cancer before we'd left our first house (he was on the operating table September 11, 2001) and died a couple of months after that so we were thrilled to bring home our second German Shepherd puppy, Timber, in 2004.

There were times when living over one hundred miles away from work made for a very long drive home. I should have bought stock in Starbucks, because caffeine was a very good friend to me. As an officer, I carried two bags of Starbucks coffee with me so I wouldn't have to drink the battery acid cheap coffee that was purchased with the station fund money. The assigned personnel paid a set amount into the fund every payday which covered essentials like coffee. And anyone who floated in for a shift pitched in a dollar. But when somebody floated in on overtime, blue shirts chipped in an extra ten and officers were expected to pay an extra twenty dollars towards dinner. I was generous with the crew, and they caught on quickly. I only had one rule: I get the first cup, no exceptions. Once, when I was lieutenant on a rescue truck, a young paramedic student showed up to ride with me. We got to talking, and I learned he just happened to work at Starbucks. Jackpot! He started bringing in bags of coffee that weren't fresh enough to sell but were still delicious, and all three shifts enjoyed this little treat much more than the donuts students usually brought in. Gifts aside, he was a good student. I hope he got hired quickly after completing his training and is now enjoying a wonderful career.

Even with the caffeine flowing, commuting wasn't easy. To mitigate the stress, I worked a lot of forty-eight-hour shifts and swapped shifts with people so that I could work a lot and then have a lot of time off, reducing my time on the road. On one particularly hectic forty-eight-hour shift, I got about two hours of sleep total. When I got off duty totally exhausted, the long drive home was both danger-ous and irresponsible, but I wanted to go home and sleep in my own bed. A few of the guys who also chose to live far from work told me they would pull over at rest stops and catch a cat nap before continuing the rest of the way home, but I didn't want to waste any of my downtime. I had the car window rolled down to help me stay alert as I drank a very large container of coffee. I don't know how I made it home in one piece. My husband was furious with me for not sleeping at the fire station before heading home. He had also experienced extreme fatigue after a crazy forty-eight-hour shift a couple of years earlier. He got T-boned when he was just a mile or so from home. He hadn't even seen the other car, and it totaled our station wagon. Luckily, he wasn't hurt. Sleep deprivation is worse than being drunk. Lesson learned.

We discussed having children, but neither one of us had the burning desire to be parents, and we didn't have family anywhere near us to help while we worked so far away. I saw the sacrifice that my own mother had made for my siblings and me, and I had such a longing for a different kind of life that I felt I could never be the kind of mother that I had been so fortunate to have. We were older by the time we married, anyway, so we chose fur kids instead. Some of our coworkers would tease us and call us "dinks"—double-income, no kids—but we would just laugh and say, "Everybody makes choices."

I, for one, know with certainty that I made the right ones for myself.

TEN

PTSD? NAH, NOT US

During a recent get-together with friends and former colleagues, we started reminiscing about calls—how they stayed in our memory banks and how we could remember exact details like smells, faces, times, and everything else. A good friend who was a skilled paramedic (though not a firefighter) was there. She was one of the original twelve people—and one of the first females—hired as paramedics in Broward County EMS before Fire and EMS merged together, and before the sheriff merged the two entities under the Broward Sheriff umbrella. Believe me, this was a group of true trailblazers. They were aggressive, and I learned a lot from watching and learning from them on calls. Talk about history.

This friend had seen her fair share of horrific calls, and as we enjoyed a meal and some wine together with our significant others that night, she suddenly turned to me and asked, "Do you think we have PTSD?"

I kind of laughed and said, "Of course, we do."

She proceeded to tell me she could hardly drive on I-95 because of her memories of all of the horrible accidents she'd responded to. I am an anxious passenger, myself, but my own fears are probably tied to a horrible school bus accident I was in as a child in wintery

Ohio. Our bus hit a car that had run a stop sign, and we rolled several times. Since there were no seatbelts, we were tossed about like ragdolls, resulting in a fatality. Though that particular traumatic memory wasn't tied to my years in the fire service, I know I have plenty that are.

If there was ever a period when our line of work gave us PTSD, it was the period after September 11. I remember reporting for shift on the twelfth, my colleagues and me gathering in the fire station sad, numb, and glued to the television just like everybody else in the world. We were in shock, and some of us knew civilians, firefighters, or cops who were lost that day. It was a tragic time for the whole country and having the eyes of the world constantly watching must have added to the stress the firefighters directly involved in the search and rescue process felt. Still, we know what we signed up for, and if it happened in any other city in America, the local firefighters would've responded the same way. In fact, our department had a special operations crew with technical rescue expertise, and they (along with crews from all over the country) headed directly to New York, where they spent a few weeks on the pile—their term for what had become of the Twin Towers.

Despite the horror, that time brought out the best in many of us. The public we served came out in droves, from every economic region of the areas we covered, to thank us. Entire classes would come by to see us at our fire stations, bringing pictures they'd drawn of firefighters and trucks. These gestures truly warmed our hearts— and filled our bellies with cookies and cakes, too. It was a unique time to be a firefighter, and we were grateful and humbled. People called us heroes—even those of us who'd stayed behind to continue serving their own hometowns—but most of us felt like we were just doing our jobs. After all, we weren't the heroes who ran up those stairs of the towers on that fateful day; we had simply continued to do what we always do, which is protect our communities as well as we could. The constant attention on our profession was a bit overwhelming, and we could only imagine what the firefighters in New York were going through.

Tragedy and trauma are the norms in this profession, but the way that we handle it is what separates those of us who are able to continue living with the ghosts in our memory banks and those for whom the traumas become debilitating. Counseling wasn't the norm back in the day, and it was kind of ridiculed, to be honest. We were firefighter-paramedics, and we were expected to be tough, competent, and ready and willing to respond to your worst day and handle the crisis to the best of our abilities. When those sirens rang out, we were supposed to take care of the situation, shake it off, and move on to the next call. we rarely talked about calls whether they were routine, strange, or funny, but especially the most traumatic ones to civilian friends or family members. We don't want them to have nightmares, too. I had a unique situation because I met my husband on the job, and we could talk to each other about it if needed. Believe me, that was a gift. But most of the people I knew and worked with didn't have that advantage and instead kept everything to themselves. We'd chosen this life, and we did our best to cope with whatever it threw at us, not second-guessing our decisions or wondering if we could've done something more or different or better. That will drive you insane. Instead, we stayed stalwart—faces brave, eyes ahead, nerves of steel fully intact.

Unfortunately, studies have now shown that some of us did suffer in silence, paying the price both physically and psychologically. That is tragic.

When I decided to take the test to become an officer, the

enormous responsibility didn't deter me, but I didn't take it lightly either. I learned to listen to advice from other people who might not be as experienced in firefighting as I was but who were construction experts or electricians or who had other important skills I lacked, such as experience in hazardous materials or technical rescue. These people were my second pair of eyes. I liked the phrase, "If you see something, say something," and I relied heavily on others who could see things I might not—or teach me how to see things I had been blind to in the past. I may have been a highly experienced firefighter by then, but I knew there was always more to learn if I wanted to make the best decisions for myself, my crew, and the people we served.

That is why ongoing training was so vital throughout my career. As new methods, techniques, equipment, and drugs were introduced, we would have to change our protocols accordingly. We went to seminars hosted by doctors in the various Broward County hospitals. We trained with different crews at the fire academy. We set up hands-on training at junkyards where we'd cut up cars and learn the newest methods to remove trauma patients. We had search-and-rescue drills at our stations, and we had mass casualty and active shooter drills at schools and the airport. We toured buildings under construction or those being torn down to see firsthand how they were built and how the materials used might react under fire conditions. We trained on gas leaks and the types of foam and application required for extinguishment. It was vital to keeps our skills current, and we knew that competence built confidence.

Toward the end of my career, I attended "Florida Fire Week," a week of hardcore classes at the fire academy close to my house. There, I trained with others on how to make entry into a building with hurricane-impact glass windows using only hand tools, how to rescue a downed firefighter in full gear, and many other things. It was intense, I was fifty-eight years old at the time, and people (my husband included) gave me grief for putting myself through such grueling training when I was so close to retirement. But I wanted to continue learning and pushing myself.

"I come by it naturally," I told the naysayers. My father was a tough old stonemason who continued working until the day he died, two days before he turned eighty-two. I must have inherited his toughness or stubbornness—or both. In general, I don't advocate working in the fire-rescue business as long as I did, but I still felt I had something to prove before retiring. I wasn't about to be "washed up" or "too old for the job." To the very end of my career, I had that hunger in my gut, and I wanted to be ready to face anything that came my way. The common saying is, "Prepare for the worst and hope for the best." It's true in the fire service, and I think this is true for most of life's quandaries, as well.

Still, all that training didn't make the job safe, and it certainly didn't protect us from the horrific sights, sounds, and smells we would encounter on a regular basis. One of the worst calls of my career happened when I was fairly new on the job and a brand-new EMT. It was a horrific fire in an old house that had been converted into an adult living facility. It was later determined that somebody had been smoking in bed and likely had fallen asleep with the cigarette still lit. Unfortunately, the fire code for nursing homes was under state-level debate at that time, and there were no required sprinklers. So when that cigarette caught, the fire spread quickly. The burn victims required fast treatment and transport for their survival, and despite our best work, there were multiple fatalities.

Upon arrival, I was ordered to assist the paramedics already on scene with patient care. One of the patients was an elderly lady whose skin was burnt and falling off. Clearly in shock, she kept repeating "What happened?" as I tried to take her vital signs. I will never forget the sight or smell of burnt flesh permeating the rescue truck that night. The scene was surreal, with multiple units flashing lights, more units arriving with sirens blaring, and bodies lined up in a row to be intubated and transported. There were only two paramedics (both female) and me, a new EMT, to handle the medical chaos. The paramedics were cool, calm, and professional, and I learned a tremendous amount from them on that day that I carried with me throughout my career. I will be forever grateful to them because they both treated me with respect and showed confidence in me and my new EMT abilities. Their assuredness was contagious, helping me stay steady and do what needed to be done. That horrible call was on-the-job training for sure.

My husband was still my new love then, and he was an acting lieutenant who was supposed to be working in the first station to respond to the fire. But, sick at home, he had called out that shift, and I have to say that I was glad he wasn't there. We were both professionals, and we both understood the risks of our jobs, but it was a different feeling to know your loved one was on a fire or a dangerous call. On days we were both working, I would listen to his calls on the radio and try to remain cool and calm. I knew he was smart and experienced, but I also knew that wouldn't always mean he was safe. I would breathe a sigh of relief every time I heard his voice on the radio saying, "Returning to quarters." He, on the other hand, didn't make it a habit to listen to my calls. He told me he trusted my judgment, and he couldn't do anything about it anyway.

I'll spare you the goriest details, but let me share a couple of other calls that didn't go the way we wanted them to. I'm not trying to depress you, and I'm certainly not after your sympathy. I just want to show you the reality of what we were up against when it came to protecting our psychological well-being.

"Engine 55, Rescue 55, respond to a cardiac arrest. CPR in progress." The call came in one Friday night after a rare, quiet dinner during which the crews had gotten to sit down and actually eat a meal while it was hot.

"Okay, guys, let's go," I said, and within minutes, the bay doors were opening and both the engine and rescue pulling out with lights on and sirens and airhorns blasting. As we drove, we listened to dispatch's updates on the radio, making sure our current routing was the fastest way to get there. We were ready to go to work, and as always, we were prepared for the worst.

The house was set back from the road in a rural area near Fort Lauderdale, called Southwest Ranches, where people could escape from the concrete jungle with land, horses, and livestock. Upon our arrival, it was all hands-on deck, and everyone grabbed a piece of equipment: stretcher, auto pulse, drug box, oxygen bag, suction, etc. The front door was already slightly ajar, and I pushed it open all the way, yelling, "Fire-rescue!"

"In here," a female voice yelled back. "In the bedroom!"

It is wise to assess your environment quickly when entering a residence and to always identify an exit just in case. There could be weapons, drugs, or angry protective dogs jeopardizing our safety. I saw none of that in this home. Rather, the first thing I smelled was delicious seafood, then the aromatic scent of candles. The dining table was set with beautiful dishes and glassware, and I heard soft jazz playing as I made my way back to the bedroom. It was apparent this was meant to be a romantic evening.

Upon entering the bedroom, I saw a very large man, naked and sprawled out on the bed. A large blonde woman knelt over him, attempting to perform CPR while crying. Okay, this was going to be labor-intensive for a lot of reasons. First, we had to get her out of the bedroom and try and get any information we could from her: what had happened and how long ago, what his medical history looked like, and whether they'd been doing any drugs prior to his collapse, for starters. She sobbed as she responded to our questions, telling us her date had come over for a romantic dinner, and afterward, they'd gone into the bedroom to continue their evening. Apparently, he'd collapsed suddenly *in the middle of things*. A scenario like this may seem cliché or like part of a bad comedy set, but for people going through it in real life, it's nothing short of traumatic. As the fire-rescue crew, it was vital that we remained professional, empathetic, and firm while this woman—or anyone we were helping—was falling apart as we did everything in our power to save her date's life.

I led the woman out of the bedroom to gather more information from her, and to give the crews more space as they moved the man to the floor to start CPR correctly on a hard surface. Working a code is controlled chaos. Adrenaline is pumping, everybody has a job to do, and if you're lucky to have a good crew with you, it is a beautiful thing to witness, despite the tragic circumstances. This kind of call is all asses and elbows, with everybody grabbing equipment, working on the patient, and putting trash into red bags as fast as they can. One crew member placed EKG electrodes on the patient's chest to see what kind of rhythm he was in while CPR was in progress. Somebody else checked out his arms to find a vein, then quickly applied a tourniquet to start an IV for drug intervention. Another crew member got out the intubation kit, blade, tube, check it to make sure it was in place correctly, and lock it down to give the patient full oxygen. Once this was all done, he was loaded onto the stretcher for transport.

Meanwhile, as the officer, I was getting information, documenting events on my computer, typing in medications, and calling the hospital to tell them we were working a code, reporting what we'd done so far and any improvements we'd seen, and letting them know I would advise on our estimated arrival time once we were en route. Two of the guys on the engine crew would stay behind to clean up, and the fire-medic from the engine would ride with us in the rescue, continuing treatment.

As we exited the house with the intubated, medicated patient on the stretcher, continuing CPR as we went, I quickly looked around at the lobster tail shells on the plates. Hearing the jazz, smelling the candles, I knew this probably wasn't going to end well. Shortly after, as we turned the patient over to the nurses and ER doctor, it became clear that despite our best efforts, there was no chance of reviving him. They pronounced the patient and recorded his time of death.

We are all professionals, and we knew we had to disconnect our personal feelings from our job. I continued filling out the report on the portable tablet, getting the required signatures while watching the nurses cover the deceased with a white sheet. Outside the room, the others cleaned the stretcher and put a fresh sheet on it for the next call, all while families sat in the waiting room crying for their loved ones. I pulled back the curtain, stepped out, and found the blonde woman sitting in a chair just outside the room, crying as she waited for information. Gently placing my hand on her shoulder, I said, "I am so sorry, we did everything we could." On the way back to the station, we all shook our heads, thinking about how that poor lady would be scarred for life.

Calls like this were never easy, of course, but they were even worse when our patients were children, as in this other memorable call.

"Rescue 55, respond to an unknown medical." It was after ten o'clock in the evening, and I had just laid down in my bunk to chill after catching up on paperwork. I got up, put my glasses on, zipped up my jumpsuit, and stepped into my work boots. "Rescue 55 responding," I said into the radio. While en route, I asked dispatch if they had any updated information. "There is a language barrier," they said, "but the patient is a little girl with a headache, and the parents don't speak English, so her brother is giving us the information."

"Copy that," I said, groaning inwardly. We were tired, grouchy, and thinking this was a bullshit call. But then dispatch came back over the radio with new information. It turned out the patient was terminal with a brain tumor. They said hospice was in the house, but when it appeared the patient was dying, the parents kicked out the hospice nurse and had their son call 911.

"Okay, copy," I said. "Rescue 55 responding."

When we arrived, I identified my crew as fire-rescue as I pushed open the door. We were met by a young Asian boy who looked to be around ten years old. He was crying, and so were his parents. They were sitting together on the couch, and they nodded to us politely as the little boy led us to the back bedroom. His sister was approximately eight years old, with translucent skin and a swollen head that was bald from chemo. We carefully assessed her and moved her gently onto our stretcher while we tried to get more information from her brother. Since he was our only source of information, I made the decision to let him ride with us to the hospital, which wouldn't usually be allowed because he was a minor. He spoke to his parents in Chinese, and they motioned for him to go with us. His parents would drive to the hospital themselves, he said. He sat on the bench seat in the back of the rescue across from his sister's stretcher, mostly quiet except when he would lean over to her, stroke her face, and whisper to her in his native language.

This call sucked, plain and simple.

This was a part of life over which we had no control, even as a trained fire-rescue crew. At this point, all we could do was watch, and that was the hardest part. But again, we had to put our feelings aside, treat the patient the best we could, and prepare for the next call. So we turned her care over to the ER doctor, left her brother with the nurse in the room, and softly told him goodbye.

This was what we signed up for. It didn't mean we never talked or cried amongst ourselves when we returned to the station. In fact, all the way back that night, we talked about how much that call sucked, and how unfair life can be.

Back at the station, I went into the office to finish the paperwork, then to my bunk to lie down. My head spun as I tried to sleep, unable to stop thinking about that little girl. Out of self-preservation, I rarely followed up on calls, but I decided to call the hospital the next morning on my long drive home.

The nurse told me the girl had passed a little while ago. I thanked her and hung up. With a few tears in my eyes, I thought about my big brother, Gary. He was my protector when I was a little girl. Nobody wanted to see or experience the wrath of "Squawman," so for the most part, bullies left me alone. I remembered when I was just in kindergarten, lying down on my mat to take a nap after a snack of milk and cookies. The fire alarm went off, so the teacher got us up and started shepherding us into a line to exit the building. Suddenly there he was: my big brother. He was only in sixth grade, but he was probably over six feet tall already. "I'm here to get my baby sister," he told the teacher before coming through the door, scooping me into his arms, and carrying me outside to safety. He then proceeded to hold me until the alarm was silenced and we could return to class. I got a lump in my throat thinking about how much I missed him, and the lump grew bigger as I thought about that sweet, stoic little boy who'd comforted his baby sister, knowing she was going to die.

No matter how well trained or how prepared we were, our calls sometimes ended in tragedy. Those were the times we really had to focus on protecting our mental health—on separating our performance from the outcome and not blaming ourselves when we'd done everything we could.

ELEVEN

MISTAKES WERE MADE

Of course, sometimes when a call got the best of us, it was our own damn fault. I was always thorough and careful—it was something I prided myself on. But a couple of times, I slipped up and got in a hurry, with consequences ranging from painful and annoying to potentially life-threatening. We all make mistakes—that is human nature—but try not to make the same one twice and try not to make mistakes like these in the first place.

Early in my career, on an engine responding to a trailer fire, I was responsible for grabbing the nozzle and entering the trailer to put the fire out. It was a double-wide in an old trailer park, and the fire was so hot that flames were shooting out of all the kitchen appliances when we entered the trailer. It flashed while we were inside putting it out, and I ended up with second-degree burns on the tops of my ears.

How did this happen, even with all my training and vigilance? Well, the simple truth is that I slipped up. I didn't have a Nomex hood on—at the time they weren't standard issue, and I hadn't bought mine yet—and the ear flaps on my helmet were not completely down.

My mistake.

My husband was on duty at another station that day, and he, too, responded to the fire I was on. When he arrived with his crew, the battalion chief immediately took him aside and told him that I had suffered burned ears but was okay and would be transported to the hospital. He was grateful for the heads up, and he trusted the chief's word that I was going to be fine. No need to freak out. If the tables had been turned and he was injured, I know that I would have responded similarly. We were both able to stay cool and calm, not panicking prematurely or getting grossed out or nauseated at horrific scenes. We had a job to do, and we were more than prepared to handle it.

Getting my ears burned was my first stupid mistake, but fortunately, the fallout was mild, all things considered. The next time I messed up like that, it would scare the living daylights out of me in more ways than one, threatening to change my life forever.

When I was stationed in western Broward County, we routinely responded to calls at a truly soulless place on the border of our district: Broward Correctional Institution, a now-defunct maximum-security prison for women. (At one time, it had housed female death row inmates, including infamous serial killer Aileen Wuornos. After BCI closed down its death row, she was transferred to another maximum-security facility and later executed at the Florida State Prison in northern Florida. Many years later, Charlize Theron won an Academy Award for playing Wuornos in the movie *Monster*.)

I hated running calls at the prison, as did most of the crews. As we moved around the facility to do our work, the inmates gave us creepy looks, talked shit to us, spouted sexual innuendo, and stared us down while licking their lips. It didn't matter if you were male or female—they were horny and hungry for new blood.

There were specific, strict rules we had to follow for our own protection, and they helped a bit. However, once we arrived at the compound, we stood by in our respective trucks and waited just outside the large metal gates topped with razor wire. Once the staff acknowledged us and opened the gates, we drove to the front of the main building and were met by a couple of burly guards. (Many of the guards we encountered there seemed cold and apathetic, even when one of their own had a medical emergency. I guess working day in and day out in that depressing place took its toll on your psyche.) We had to leave our radios, badges, pens, name tags, and wallets in the engine and rescue trucks so the inmates couldn't steal them and use them as weapons. All we could bring in were our IDs, which we placed into the bulletproof drawer located just inside the foyer, along with a list of the names, ranks, and unit numbers of everyone on our crew. This way, there was a record in case something bad happened to us.

Once we were checked in, a guard would escort us to the elevator and ride with us to the medical floor. As we walked down the hallways, we could see into the small rooms on each side, where inmates were receiving their medications or talking to counselors, doctors, or whomever they needed to see. They even had a small ER room. Sounded like a good setup for us to swoop into when needed, but this floor was staffed by the latest doc-in-a-box, who wasn't always that attentive, so on every call, we reassessed the patient, sometimes start an IV, and administer medication as needed to stabilize them. Then, we'd transport them to the hospital, handcuffed to our stretcher with a guard sitting on the bench seat across from them.

We were never told what our patients' crimes were, though we often looked them up on the public website later. One way to get a clue as to the severity of their criminal background was to count how many unmarked vans followed us to the hospital. Three was usually a very bad sign, and a docile patient who looked like someone's grandmother would often turn out to be a vicious murderer.

The hospital we transported these patients to was in an affluent area in southwest Broward County, so you can only imagine the terrified looks from nurses, doctors, patients, and visitors seeing someone handcuffed to the stretcher and accompanied by an armed officer. The kicker was always when the vans pulled up and the guards got out carrying shotguns. They would try to be inconspicuous, but subtlety was never their strong suit.

This particular Saturday, we'd had nonstop calls on top of torrential rain and lightning out of an old-school horror movie. So we were already exhausted when the medical call came in at almost midnight for a seizure at the prison. We responded with the engine crew, but we were escorted to the women's dormitory instead of the medical floor. Have you ever watched the old prison movies where the inmates, in bunks stacked three-high, start rising from their beds when the door opens? Well, I hate to be dramatic, but this was just like that.

The patient was in the bathroom in the back of the dormitory, still actively seizing. Our safety is paramount on any call, anywhere, and we knew that if the inmates started a riot, we could find ourselves stuck with them in a lockdown situation until additional security guards and police arrived. So we quickly carried her out of the bathroom and out of the dorm, where we put her on the stretcher to start treatment immediately.

We were all crammed together underneath the building's tiny overhang, rain pouring down as we tried to keep her from jumping off the stretcher. It was a terrible situation. Everybody was scrambling to get the IV ready, place a tourniquet, and hold her down to administer medication to stop the seizures. Someone handed me a needle to put into the small red sharps container. In a hurry, I pushed the needle into the opening without looking, stopping cold when I felt a sharp pain in my hand. I'd been stuck.

Shit! You thought getting my ears burned was dumb? Well, pardon my language, but this was a *real fucking rookie mistake!*

The battalion chief was immediately notified, and we were taken out of service after dropping the patient off at the hospital. Per protocol, if the needle you got stuck with was the patient's, then the patient could agree to have it tested for HIV or any other nasty disease that you may have just contracted. But this wasn't my night, and we couldn't be sure which of the dozens of needles in the sharps container had been the culprit, which meant we couldn't positively identify it as the patient's. So the nightmare began.

Imagine your life, hopes, and dreams flashing before your eyes. Mine did.

In no time at all, I was sitting on a bed in the ER at busy Broward General hospital, listening to the doctor advising me to start an anti-viral treatment within twenty-four hours. He rattled off all of the terrible side effects I could expect, and then he handed me a stack of papers to sign acknowledging all the risks—including the risk that the treatment wouldn't work and I would still contract HIV, hepatitis, or some other nasty disease. It was 2:30 a.m., and I was exhausted and terrified. I knew the first person I needed to call. The most important person in my life, whom I loved dearly, was most likely sound asleep at home, over one hundred miles away, and would be getting up in a couple of hours to drive south for his shift.

I called him anyway.

I told him what had happened and relayed everything the doctor had said, including the unpleasant and potentially dangerous side effects that made me hesitant about starting the regimen. He listened to everything I said, and then he shocked me back to reality with just five words.

"Do you want to die?"

Smooth talker, my husband.

I said no, of course, not.

"Well, then, you don't have a choice, do you?" he replied.

Dammit! He had a way of cutting through the bullshit, and he wasn't about to let me get away with feeling sorry for myself. He knew I was scared, and frankly, he probably was too, but he wouldn't say it. He had always been my biggest advocate, but he never candy-coated the truth, even when I didn't want to hear it.

I was frightened, but my husband was absolutely right, so that was that. I got to work.

I took nine huge horse pills every day for a month. I'll spare you the ugly details, but the side effects were every bit as nasty as the doctor had warned me they might be. Let's just say food poisoning would have been a welcome exchange.

The one plus side of these horrific side effects is that they probably saved my beloved German shepherd, Timber, that Christmas Eve. My husband had baked two large cranberry pecan pies, and while they were cooling on the kitchen countertop, we borrowed our neighbor's golf cart, which he always decorated to the nines for Christmas, to hand out presents and toast the holiday with our neighbors. Well, while we were out, my stomach started churning, and there was no way to stop it. We raced back to the house in the golf cart. I jumped off and ran into the bathroom, but my husband immediately noticed that Timber had eaten one of the pies and was getting ready to chow down on the other one. Dogs cannot process sugar, and he developed a huge hematoma on his right flank. We took him to the vet immediately, where we learned that if he had succeeded in eating the second pie, he probably would have died.

As part of my regimen, I visited the county infectious disease doctor close to my house. He was brilliant and a lifesaver, soothing my anxiety and answering all my questions in such a professional manner. A tall, thin gentleman with wild gray hair and a foreign accent, he reminded me of Doc Brown from *Back to the Future.*

After that first month of pills, I got tested for a variety of diseases regularly over the course of a year: once a week for the first month, then once a month for three months after that, then again three months later, and one final time a year after this all started. Walking into the county facility for infectious diseases was quite a humbling experience. I'd sit on a threadbare chair in the dark, dank waiting room next to people showing the physical signs of AIDs and God only knew what else. Realizing most of them probably suffered from a lack of basic healthcare, I came to be more grateful than ever for the healthcare choices and access I had in my own adult life. I always kept my bare arms folded in my lap so I wouldn't have to touch anything with my skin, but thankfully, I never had to sit in that waiting room long before a nurse would motion for me to come through the door.

Fortunately, I was declared healthy and disease-free after the last test, but I learned a valuable lesson that year. Life is indeed precious, and your rushed choices can change your life in a nanosecond.

TWELVE

ENEMAS, HOARDERS, AND RED-BOTTOMED HEELS

In every call I ran—especially those that were physically or emotionally difficult, I did my best to follow three rules. I learned the first two in EMT school and the third in the fire academy:

1. This is not our crisis or emergency.

2. Stress is what you create for yourself.

3. Be aware, because if the rescuer goes down, who will rescue the rescuer?

These rules helped me keep my head in the game and focus on my goal, which was to prevent tragedy. They were particularly important when I became an officer, first as a lieutenant and later as a captain, and began floating into one big, busy station that housed a ladder truck with four people, an engine with three, two rescues with three people each, and a battalion chief. Most of the people assigned to this station were ambitious, used to the pace, and comfortable with the area—or else they were young and assigned there whether they wanted it or not. I would often take the overtime shift the day after my regular shift because nobody else wanted it—not at this particular house, anyway. So by the time it became apparent, usually by noon, that nobody was going to pick up the overtime, I knew I might as well settle in for another twenty-four hours, take the money, and prepare to be up all night.

The territory this house served was a cornucopia of different types of occupancies, including nursing homes, rehab centers, section-eight housing, drug rehab housing, gang territories, and ancient condos full of senior citizens on fixed incomes. There was a particularly diverse area within the territory that we not-so-affectionately called Epcot. It consisted of drug rehab houses, gangs, and a four-lane, north-south highway called 441.

During one of the many busy shifts I worked at this station, we responded to four "sevens"—calls in which we'd arrive to find the patient beyond any kind of human intervention—in twenty-four hours. This was a strange shift indeed. Although it wasn't unusual to respond to nursing homes where the patient was a seven, having four in one shift was not the norm. And they were not usually due to trauma, but age, illness, and disease had taken its toll on them. But trauma due to motor vehicle accidents was another unforgiving situation. One particularly notable signal seven occurred on northbound Powerline Road in Pompano. The victim had driven his car right underneath a semi-truck that had turned onto the road in front of him. And upon our arrival, it was apparent that his injuries were incompatible with life. He was dead; he had, in fact, been decapitated. Both hands were still clutching the steering wheel, but his head was sitting in the back seat. It was a macabre sight, to say the least. We found out from the cops on the scene that the victim had been drinking heavily at the strip club a few miles down the road and then proceeded to get behind the wheel. Knowing the circumstances, we were grateful he didn't kill any innocent people, and we felt terrible for the poor truck driver who was just trying to make his way home after a long day.

Sevens were tough since, by definition, there was nothing we could do for our patients. But these calls still required that I contact law enforcement, inform any family members on the scene, and write reports—in between running other calls and trying to scarf down some food. The pace was nuts, but you learned to run on pure adrenaline and suck it up.

I know that sounds callous, but as I've mentioned, being able to separate ourselves from the tragedy was a critical part of the job. Still, though, this profession teaches you all kinds of lessons about the human psyche if you stick around long enough and pay attention.

I'll never forget another call that came in during a shift at this busy station. More specifically, I will never forget the weary look I saw on the young woman's face when we responded to an unknown medical call in her mother's rundown condo building. When we knocked, a squat old woman opened the door and immediately started screaming, "I need an enema!" over and over. Standing behind her was a tall, skinny blonde woman, presumably her daughter, who looked as though she'd been browbeaten since birth. Well, enemas weren't in our job description, but we did need to calm her down enough to check her vital signs and obtain a medical history. Her daughter told us she was agitated that she couldn't poop but refused to take a laxative. This is a common problem with old people who are taking buckets of medications and consuming no fiber and hardly any water (even though they swear to you, they drink it all day long).

No matter what we said, the old woman just continued screaming at us about needing an enema, so I knew the only way to handle her was to transport her to the hospital. The daughter was visibly relieved as we loaded her mother onto the stretcher for transport. "Are you going to ride in with us?" I asked her. She declined, saying she'd drive her car to the hospital. By the look on her face, I thought she might just keep on driving, and frankly, I wouldn't have blamed her.

This wasn't the first time I'd seen that combination of worry and relief on an overburdened relative's face. Sometimes people called because they were just exhausted from taking care of their loved ones. Other times, they needed their medications, a hot shower, or a meal but didn't have the means or the wherewithal to take care of themselves. Being in the fire-rescue business means going out of your way to help others in need, even if it's just to get them a fast-food sandwich or make them a peanut butter and jelly sandwich from their own home because their blood sugar was low, and they didn't want to go to the hospital.

Most of the time, it seemed people waited to call us until three o'clock in the morning, otherwise known as the bewitching hour. Sometimes it was a true emergency, and in some cases, waiting had turned a solvable problem into a tragedy. But no matter the hour, there were some calls that just made me shake my head in disbelief. Here's a sampling:

A. The teenagers who put green or brown Anoles on their ears like earrings and couldn't remove them.

B. The hysterical lady who got her fingers caught in the toaster.

C. The young man wearing a Superman T-shirt who called

us because there was a small snapping turtle in his garage. (When contained and relocated easily to the canal across the street, the caller's girlfriend was more impressed with the cute firefighters than she was with him.)

There are also genuine, legitimate calls that no doubt embarrass the caller but don't faze us. As a crew, we have really seen it all, and our job is to serve without judgment. One poor old man got his balls stuck between the slats of a lawn chair. He was understandably mortified, but we just fixed the problem while trying to save his dignity. Another man fell through his shower door and had shards of glass implanted all over his backside, so we transported him face down on the stretcher, covered with a sheet. Homeless people called because they were cold, hungry, and just wanted a shower. I responded to medical calls where the patients were hoarders, and it was truly like a maze trying to gain access to them. One guy was in the living room sitting in his recliner and had been unable to get up for a couple of days. The entire apartment had newspapers stacked from the floor to the ceiling. That is a true fire hazard, not to mention a logistical nightmare.

Sometimes, we didn't know what we were facing until we got there. Dispatchers have a great responsibility to get as much information as they can from a caller, and I commend them for what they do, but between callers' hysteria, any language barriers, and frequent background noise, it's a tough job. Sometimes, this means the situation is completely different from what the dispatcher prepared you for. I learned to be somewhat of a detective in the questions I would ask them en route, but there was no way to eliminate the chaos altogether in an emergency situation.

But whatever we encountered in a call—however surprising

it may have been—our job was to serve the people who needed our help, and I genuinely felt called to do just that. I'd run calls on people who really needed our services but hesitated because they didn't have any insurance or on elderly patients who refused transport because they feared they would never see their home again. (Sometimes they were right.) While I did have to keep my own emotions separate, I strove to approach every patient or fire victim with understanding instead of judgment.

One night, I learned that lonely people sometimes call 911 just to talk to someone. It was almost midnight, and I was working on a rescue with two other people, one of whom was a competitive bodybuilder with a degree in nutrition and a megawatt smile. The other was a woman who had worked at the worst stations in downtown Fort Lauderdale when Broward Fire and Broward EMS were separate. She once told me she had helped deliver more than a few dozen babies to young girls living in the ghetto.

The call came in as "unknown medical," and when the dispatcher gave the address, the guy on my truck said, "Oh, I know that woman." Apparently, he'd run on her many times, and she had a history of anxiety, so he'd given her his cell phone number to call him so he could calm her down instead of tying up 911. (Talk about going above and beyond.) We arrived at the address, and I was amazed to see this woman lived in a mansion—the polar opposite of what I'd envisioned when my partner told us about her.

Upon entering, though, I noticed there were a few strange-looking people inside, which kind of threw me off. The patient was a young woman, and she was very nice and apologetic. We assessed her vitals, the guy on my truck calmed her down, and we sat with her for a while. She kept offering us her house, saying we could move in and live with her rent-free. I thought that was strange and sad, but as I looked around, I started to put the pieces together. I noticed all of these high heels lying on the floor, every single one of them with iconic red bottoms. As a fashion lover and former model, I knew those shoes: Christian Louboutins. They were probably worth upward of a thousand dollars each, and they'd just been thrown about the floor like they were from Walmart. As I studied the shoes and listened to this woman pleading with us to move into her mansion, I realized why these weird-looking people were hanging around. They were vagabonds she'd befriended somewhere, and they were more than happy to use her for a free ride until they moved on.

After we left the patient's house, we got the scoop. She was from a very wealthy family, and her grandparents had left her with a few million dollars. She'd hooked up with a baseball player and gotten pregnant. Then he'd left her, and now she lived all alone in this gigantic house. She was lonely, and she had developed a reputation for picking up stray people, many of whom were more than happy to take advantage of her situation by leeching off both her hospitality and her money. I couldn't help but feel incredibly sad for her. Most of us worked hard and still couldn't comprehend being that rich. Having grown up dirt-poor, I appreciate having nice things, but this woman really drove home the hard-to-believe adage that money can't buy happiness. I couldn't help but wonder if her inheritance had been a bit of a curse. Unfortunately, once we'd determined the patient was physically fine, there was nothing we could do for her; mental health services were outside of our authority, unless she was deemed mentally incompetent. In that case, we would be called to transport her to a psychiatric ward after family members, cops, or a doctor imposed a Baker Act. We couldn't legally do that.

Another one I can't forget is the old man who lived behind the Church's Chicken joint on Sunrise Boulevard. A double amputee, he was in a wheelchair, and we would occasionally buy him a burger and fries because he didn't like the greasy chicken from Church's. He told us he'd gotten hit by a city bus and was just waiting for his ship to come in with a big settlement so he could afford a place to live. He also told us his relatives lived close by but they were after his money, so he preferred to stay behind the chicken joint. We offered several times to contact social services for him, but he always declined our offer, saying his money was coming soon. The last time we ran on him, he had maggots in both of his stumps. I covered them with red medical waste bags and secured them both with tape. The smell was so horrid that I grabbed my air pack before riding into the hospital with the rescue crew. I'm sure I was a sight, opening the doors of the ER in my air pack and face mask to wheel him in on the stretcher. We never saw him again, so I guess unfortunately his ship did come in, just not the way he thought it would.

There were funny calls that we laughed about later in the privacy of the station, and there were terrible ones that made us want to cry. But when we approached them all with empathy (not sympathy, because that puts us in emotional whitewater), and we followed the three critical rules, then we were able to do our best work serving those who need our help.

THIRTEEN

ANIMALS, DRUNKS, AND PORN

One Friday night, I was working in a double-wide on wheels that housed a rescue and an engine company with three of my favorite people on it. Behind our double-wide was a portable that served as a volunteer station. Most of the volunteers were decent, dedicated men and women, and some were trying to get hired by a paid department. But sometimes their proximity to our station created friction because the volunteers would attempt to take charge if they beat us to a scene.

I was a captain at this point, still floating all over the county since I didn't have enough seniority to be able to bid a station. I enjoyed working with different people and running calls in different areas, and I adored the lieutenant who worked at this particular station. He was extremely knowledgeable and had a great sense of humor. Whenever I saw he was on duty, I breathed a sigh of relief, because I knew I could count on him and his crew no matter what crazy calls might come our way. Sure enough, the first call that came in on this particular Friday night was like none I had ever responded to.

Animals have always held a very special place in my heart. In fact, sometimes I prefer them to humans. They are four-legged angels with fur. So, when I learned this call was about a hit and run with a unique victim—a horse—my stomach dropped. But off we went, both engine and rescue, listening to vague updates about whether the horse or the person who hit him was still on scene. In this rural area, there are no streetlights, and most of the roads are unpaved.

When we arrived, along with a police car, we got out of our respective vehicles with flashlights in our hands. It didn't take us long to locate the horse. He was lying on the side of the muddy road, moaning, with blood everywhere. It was heartbreaking to witness. This huge horse's body had suffered lots of trauma, and it was clear there was nothing we could do for our patient. The police officer said he was going to put the horse out of its misery, and as hard as that was to hear, we all knew that it was the humane thing to do. We slowly walked over to the horse one last time, talking softly to this once-majestic animal. "It will be okay, buddy," we whispered. All of us tough firefighters reduced to tears, we turned away to give the officer space, flinching when we heard the gunshot.

A witness came forward and said the horse belonged to their neighbors across the street. They had left earlier to go to dinner, and the horse must have gotten out of the gate. The witness heard the car hit it and ran outside in time to write down the license plate and call 911. Sure enough, a few minutes later, as we followed a bloody trail to the fence where the horse had made its fateful escape, we saw headlights coming toward us. The owners had returned from dinner. They both started crying when we told them what had happened, and they made their way over to pay respects to their beautiful horse.

In the meantime, the police had located the car and driver responsible: a teenage kid. His father was also contacted, and both of them were on their way back to the scene of the accident so the kid could take responsibility for his actions. Luckily for us, our work was done, and we returned to our quarters. But it was only the beginning of an ominous night.

A couple of hours later, we responded to another horrible call: a car in the canal on Griffin Road. We knew the area well and prepared for the worst. The deep canal ran east to west along the busy two-lane road, and people drove along it like they were Mario Andretti on a damn racetrack, regardless of rain or fog. We responded frequently to terrible car and ATV accidents in and around the canal and given the hour of night and the steady rain, we knew this one wouldn't likely be good.

Upon arrival, we first spotted the paddy wagon that the police had set up, and then we spotted the car in the canal. The driver, however, was standing on the side of the road being interrogated by the numerous police on scene. He had been speeding and almost ran another car off the road, scaring the hell out of a nineteen-year-old girl who'd been driving home from work. The cops on scene had already decided he was going to jail. He was obviously shit-faced, so I was on board with that decision, but it was our job to make sure he got checked out and transported to the hospital according to our department protocols. I never liked going toe-to-toe with the cops because I respected the hell out of most of them, and I was thankful to have them respond prior to our arrival to secure the scene in many dicey situations. But I wasn't about to let them throw this asshole in the back of a police car or paddy wagon where he could die from an undiagnosed injury. Even though he'd almost killed a young girl, he had to be checked out and transported to the hospital for clearance before going to jail. After all, his inebriation could mask a traumatic brain injury. An oversight like that could cost me my job and my license, and I could be personally sued or possibly jailed myself. So I stood my ground.

After a much heated discussion, we went ahead and plugged the patient with an IV, which meant there would be no possibility of turning him over to the police first. They were pissed at me, to say the least, and they didn't hesitate to tell me so, but I didn't care. Even my naïve partner, who was new and green said to me, "He's just drunk. What a bummer that he can't just go home." She had a lot to learn.

The patient's parents arrived on scene shortly thereafter, and it became apparent that this wasn't his first rodeo. They thanked me and my partner profusely for taking care of him, and a firefighter who knew him later confirmed that this was not the first time he'd been caught driving under the influence, so it was only a matter of time before he killed someone. Well, at least the innocent girl he'd almost hit that night wasn't his first victim. Unfortunately, the drunks usually survive with nary a scratch while the innocent ones are maimed or killed.

Now, before you go thinking life in fire-rescue is one tragedy after another, let me share a couple of the more *curious* calls I responded to. After all, not every call is a heartbreak. Some are just damn hard to believe. But, as they say, truth is stranger than fiction. Here's one that turned out to be like a slutty B-movie on late-night television.

"What the fuck kind of crazy, demented place is this?" I said to the other firefighter as we dragged the hose line back out of the house after putting out the fire. The call had come in as a structure fire, and we'd responded as usual, adrenaline pumping through our veins as we anticipated how big the fire would be. Soon, the telling column of smoke in the distance confirmed this one was going to be a thrill. But just what kind of thrill we were in for, we had no way to predict. We could tell this place was different as soon as we arrived, just by observing who was wandering around the scene.

And as we made our way through the different rooms once the fire was out and overhaul had started, things just got weirder. There were dildos everywhere. Some were attached to mannequins. Some of the mannequins were hanging from the ceiling by ropes that were tied around their necks. Hell, there were mannequins hanging from the showerheads in the bathrooms, all with anatomically correct dildos sticking out like large appendages.

This was a sex house.

This was definitely a new experience for me.

The people living in this crazy house were outside, eyeing us like fresh meat or candy just waiting to be devoured. My lieutenant was a gorgeous guy in incredible shape, with a big smile; dark, curly hair; and limitless charisma. They were hooting and hollering explicit details of just what they would like to do to him—and the rest of us, too. But he just smiled back at them as we repacked the large-diameter hose into the hose bed. We kept our heads down and did our job, gathering all of the equipment so we could get out of there and turn the scene over to the fire marshal.

Unfortunately for the residents, but fortunately for my colleagues, this house would reignite the next two days in a row, finally burning to the ground on the third day. To this day, we don't know what caused the first, but all three shifts got to see the weird sex house firsthand.

Here's another one, more like a B-rated horror movie than a skin flick. I was working as a lieutenant on a rescue truck when a call came over the radio describing an unknown foul odor. The address was a Section 8 apartment complex just up the street from the station near the infamous "Swap Shop." I'd seen several fires there, along with shootings, stabbings, and medical emergencies.

This place ran the gamut of calls, so we were expecting a bloody, nasty situation.

Residents frequently hung out in the hallways of the complex, and just like clockwork, they were waiting to point us in the direction of the smell when we arrived. Of course, we didn't need much guidance, as the odor was filtering into the hallway outside the offending apartment. As we got close, we asked a few of the residents if they knew who lived there, and if so, when they had seen the tenants last. They told us that a couple with children lived there, but nobody had seen the family in a few days. That couldn't be good.

We braced ourselves before entering, prepared to see bodies, but when we forced open the locked door, we were met with a truly eerie sight. The apartment smelled like death but was otherwise immaculate, empty except for a few items. Several suitcases stood upright in the middle of the living room floor like they were ready to go somewhere. We started checking out all of the rooms, looking under the beds that had been left behind and opening the closets.

Nothing.

The scariest thing was the cradle that still had a sheet and baby blanket in it. Creeped out, we approached the cradle and moved the blanket, hoping against hope that this wouldn't be the source of the smell. Nothing. Thank goodness.

Well, the last thing we checked was the refrigerator, and we half expected to see chopped-up body parts at this point because the smell was so bad. We cautiously opened the door. Empty.

Okay. Now the freezer.

Oh, my God.

There it was: rotting fish.

Thank God it wasn't human bodies, and thank God it wasn't our responsibility to remove them from the freezer.

Once the place was secured, and we'd notified the building manager and returned to the station, all we could do was laugh, grateful it wasn't the chainsaw massacre we'd expected. We never found out what had happened to the occupants, though I imagine they'd just skipped out on the rent and hit the road. It was a relief to not find bloodied bodies, or worse, parts, though those calls happen, too. It just goes to show that you can never assume anything when a call comes through dispatch. The best course of action is to be prepared for the worst and hope for the best.

This next one was a call to remember and an important reminder of why it's important to always be on your game. I'd taken an overtime shift on Engine 67, which covers the city of Weston, located on the edge of the Everglades in southwest Broward County. This was a so-called "slow" station, and that reputation can fool you into complacency, but I knew better than to fall for it. And on that day, I'm glad I didn't.

Around noon, we got a call to respond to a truck leaking fluid—unknown product, unknown amount—on US Highway 27, which runs north and south from Miami to Tallahassee. It's a common route for semis, and it's also a commonplace for people to drive the wrong way, hitting bikers and motorcyclists and causing deadly accidents. It didn't help that the truck stop had an outside tiki bar that was jammed on the weekends.

Upon arrival, the lieutenant and I, in full gear, saw a large box truck with a visible leak flowing out of the back roll-up door. Once we opened it up, we discovered it was full of batteries, and the incident suddenly became much bigger than we could handle. We called hazmat, but their station was on the east side of town, so it would take them a while to arrive.

Rescues and a battalion chief were on their way as well. So, along with the police officers, we put down cones and shut down the northbound lanes, then settled in to wait for the cavalry.

The rescue units arrived, and at first, they parked behind the engines. But shortly afterwards, they were asked to move into the swale that divided the highway instead. The battalion chief arrived soon after and positioned his car behind the engine I was assigned to.

It just so happened that a small city's department had just merged with ours, so the on-duty battalion chief was driving a couple of their chiefs around to show them the territory. The new chiefs were curious about the area around the highway and wanted to take a look at the woods and terrain, so they all got out and walked over to the right side of the car, deep in conversation about the Everglades.

I decided to say hello to the lieutenant, who was sitting in one of the other engines parked behind ours, while the hazmat crew took care of the leaking batteries in the box truck.

Lights were flashing from all of the units on scene, cones were obvious to anybody driving north, and police officers were diverting any traffic headed our way.

And yet.

I turned around and saw a semi barreling down the highway toward us. It looked like everything was in slow motion.

"Oh, shit!" I yelled.

Everyone turned to look at what I was seeing and jumped or ran quickly out of the way. The semi kept coming and smashed into the battalion chief's car, tossing it into the air and totaling it before the police could stop it.

The "what ifs" were plenty, so all I can say is there must have been an intervention by a higher power that day.

A. What if the battalion chief and the officers he was driving around had stayed in the car?

B. What if the police couldn't get the driver to stop, and he'd taken out the other engines, too?

C. What if the rescue trucks hadn't been reassigned to park in the swale?

D. What if I hadn't happened to look back to see the whole thing unfolding before me?

I would've been waffled, along with many others on the scene. This call was the talk of the department for years to come, and the new chiefs that had been riding along that day never forgot their induction into our department.

When you're working in fire-rescue, every call is different—and some calls are *very* different. But what I came to learn is that no matter how ridiculous or how simple an event might seem, every single one deserves the same seriousness, attention, and preparation. After all, you never know when your life and your crew's lives could be at stake.

FOURTEEN

THERE BUT FOR THE GRACE OF GOD

For all the calls that scared the daylights out of me or made me want to cry, there were just as many that reminded me of just how charmed my life actually was. I had had my fair of hardships—don't get me wrong—but I had created an incredible life for myself, including a fulfilling career, a wonderful husband, financial stability, and good health. It was easy to take these things for granted, losing sight of them in light of minor inconveniences or complaints. But every once in a while, I would respond to a call that put all of my privileges in stark relief, making me grateful all over again for everything I have.

One such call happened early in my career, when I was a brand-new EMT riding backward on an engine. We were called to respond to a fall injury. The patient's name was Betty.

"Fire department!" we yelled, as always, while banging on the door.

"She's in here!" bellowed a male voice from inside. He didn't open the door for us—didn't even get up as far as I could tell. Just bellowed directions from the comfort of his recliner. "She's down the hall."

We made our way through the house, which reeked of rot and mildew, until we found Betty, an elderly woman, lying in the hall. She was in terrible condition and unable to get up. I was shocked and livid to see her in such a state while her disgusting husband sat relaxed, unconcerned, in the other room.

"I'm so sorry to make you all have to come out here," said our patient. Tears streamed down the old woman's withered face as she spoke. She told us she had fallen several hours earlier and couldn't get up. I knelt down next to her, breathing through my mouth as the smell of feces and urine (her own) and rotten food (presumably from the kitchen but permeating the whole house), assaulted my senses.

Our crew, two men and me, tried our best to be nonchalant and professional as we tended to Betty's injuries. Her deteriorating condition far predated her fall, apparently caused by inevitable aging but exacerbated by neglect. Betty said she was eighty years old, but she looked about a hundred and eighty. Her soft blue eyes, with a little spark still in them, hinted that she was someone who had fought hard just to survive her miserable lot in life. I gently cleaned the blood off of her face and scrawny arms, growing more horrified by the moment as her fat, ugly husband just sat in his ratty old recliner in the living room, watching TV, surrounded by empty Budweiser cans. He mumbled something to the effect of, "I tried to help her up, but I couldn't."

"You sorry son of a bitch," I wanted to say. "Why didn't you call us sooner and at least have the decency to clean her up?" As I looked around the house at the squalor surrounding us, I became so infuriated I wanted to punch him in his ugly bulbous nose. He obviously hadn't missed too many meals—dirty dishes overflowed from the kitchen sink, and more had spilled onto the floor. The cracked and dirty linoleum was covered in newspapers, dog poop, and vomit, likely from the mangy little rat dog who kept trying to rub up against me, wagging his tail. I didn't know if he was happy to see us and hoping to get rescued from this hell or just happy to have survived another day without becoming dinner.

Time seemed to stand still when the rescue crew finally arrived. They walked in and gasped, holding their noses, then walked right back out to wait by the stretcher. Talk about rude and disrespectful. I know they had seen worse, so why all the drama? I waded through the piles of clothes on the bedroom floor in search of a housecoat and a pair of shoes for Betty so she could cover herself up. We tried to maintain her dignity while we carried her matchstick frame outside and gently placed her onto the stretcher.

Through all of that, Betty's husband stayed put in the recliner, now with a cable guide in one hand and a beer in the other. He hardly noticed us leaving, giving nothing more than a grunt when we told him she would be at North Broward.

As the rescue crew wheeled Betty out to the truck to transport her to the hospital, we, the engine crew, glanced at each other with tired, knowing eyes. I thought of how I would want my mother to be treated if 911 was called, and this wasn't it. This was another family who had fallen through the cracks of life.

Calls like this always broke my heart, and more importantly, they always reminded me to be grateful for my relatively comfortable life—especially, in this particular case, my loving husband, who was the polar opposite of Betty's. I tried not to feel sorry for the people I served, but as often as possible, I allowed what little I knew of their stories to reignite my appreciation for my own.

Another call that has stuck with me all these years, and for similar reasons, wasn't a trauma call, only a civil assist. There was no indication, at the onset of this call, that it would be one of life's little lessons, but the young guy involved taught me a valuable lesson in empathy, humility, and civility.

As our truck plowed through a foot of water that had accumulated on the road en route to the patient's house, my only thought was a selfish one: *God, I hope I don't have to get my feet wet.*

We had just finished dinner at the station, and true to Florida summer weather, a torrential downpour was accompanying us on our call. I was sitting backward in the open cab's jump seat, with my feet tucked under me and my bunker coat over me, covering as much of myself as possible to avoid getting completely soaked before we even got to the call.

When we arrived, the patient's girlfriend let us in and led us to the living room. There he was, lying upside down on the floor of the apartment, molded to his wheelchair and twisted like a pretzel with his feet up in the air. His eyes were directed at the ceiling, and his faithful dog's angry barks warned us to stay away from his helpless master.

As we lifted the young man upright again, I noticed how handsome he was, with long, dirty blond hair and big blue eyes.

Then, I noticed his gratitude. What had been an easy maneuver for us had likely been a defining, mortifying, and maybe even life-changing moment for him, and he handled it with incredible grace. "I am paralyzed from the waist down," he said softly before thanking us profusely for our help.

His girlfriend, in total contrast to Betty's good-for-nothing husband, was by the young man's side the whole time, and she was so apologetic. "I'm so sorry I had to call you guys," she said, "but I wasn't able to get him upright by myself." The last thing we needed from this sweet young couple—or anybody we helped—was an apology, and we told them as much. "That's okay," we said. "You call us anytime you need help."

We checked him out to make sure he wasn't injured, and as we made our exit, reality hit all of us like a ton of bricks. I had been feeling uncomfortably full from having stuffed myself with a delicious dinner. I had been worried about getting my feet wet. I had been annoyed by the rain. And suddenly it occurred to me that none of that mattered.

What really mattered was that I could properly feed myself, walk in the rain, and run on the beach with my dog. I climbed back into the jump seat, declining the lieutenant's offer to let me squeeze into the cab with them. As we drove back to the station in the pouring rain, I got soaked, feet and all. Only this time, I felt incredibly lucky.

FIFTEEN

THE PUS BUS;
RUNNING ON EMPTY

I never thought I would become a paramedic. I admired those who did, but being an EMT was enough for me—or so I thought. When it became clear that, in order to move up the ranks, I had to go to paramedic school, I stepped up to the challenge. It wouldn't be easy, especially living one hundred miles away, but I already had fifteen years as an EMT under my belt, and I was assigned to an engine company that had once been the ninth busiest in the country. I could handle anything.

Inspired, my husband decided to join me at paramedic school. We had five-by-seven index cards with drug names, calculations, indications, EKG rhythms, treatments needed, and anything else we needed to know, and we would use them to quiz each other in the car. I even remember him waking me up in the middle of the night one night to ask me to tell him about the heart, blood, and circulation. Are you kidding me? I did it grudgingly, knowing he was trying to push me and make me a better paramedic. Then I went back to sleep. While in many ways having a husband who was going through this with me made the challenge a lot easier to handle, he was also infuriating! He was a natural. He never studied, but he was always in the top five of our class, shrugging it off and saying it was just because he was an engine medic. Sometimes I wanted to slap him, but for the sake of our relationship, I refrained.

Stress was part of the game in our career, as you've seen. But when your stress is about your own life rather than a stranger's, it can take hold of you in a totally different way. The curriculum was exhausting, and I struggled with it, especially since I was now commuting over a hundred miles for shift, had been married ten years, had a dog, and was a first-time homeowner living in a flood zone and working in a very busy firehouse. And on top of that, my mother was dying in the hospital in Ohio.

When my husband and I flew up to see her, we had to take all of our books so we could keep up with our studies, and we could only stay for a week at a time, or we would be kicked out of the program. She died shortly after we returned from that too-quick trip. We flew back to Florida a couple of days before Halloween, and she died that morning. When we got the news a couple of days later, I was devastated, but I also found myself re-energized to put my all into paramedic training. My mom had only had a sixth-grade education—rheumatic fever had led her to drop out of school—and I know she was proud of me for continuing my education and sticking with a tough-yet-fulfilling career choice.

I got through it all with the help of my husband; colleagues; some seasoned, generous, patient paramedics; and plain, old sweat equity. Not to mention on-the-job training—learning the protocols, seeing firsthand how things work, getting in there to handle the calls, and learning from my mistakes. These are the kind of lessons you just can't learn from reading a book.

Of course, paramedic school offered plenty of hands-on lessons, too. One in particular was about human anatomy and the trauma our bodies can suffer, which I witnessed when our instructor offered us the opportunity to see an autopsy. He told our class that it wasn't mandatory, and that he would understand if some of us just couldn't stomach it. But I wasn't squeamish, and neither was my husband, so I was excited about it in a rather curious way. Besides, what better way to actually see the liver, kidneys, brain, heart, and other internal organs up close? So, we decided to embrace the opportunity, making a plan to head to the county morgue.

When we arrived, we walked into a nondescript warehouse and signed in before entering the morgue, where there was a huge glass plate window separating us from the actual autopsy area. I immediately thought about all of the morgues I'd seen on forensic TV shows. This looked just like those, only bigger. I took in the sight: men, women—Black, brown, and White—looked eerily at peace despite the jarring sound of saws and different tools—some commonly used by your local butcher—cutting, sawing, prying, and spreading. Undeterred, they worked steadily on the bodies laid out before them in rows on steel tables, heads elevated on curved blocks to keep their necks straight. Each table had a scale hanging from a chain next to it, set up to weigh organs as they were removed.

The doctors wore white coats with colorful caps on their heads, talking among themselves. But the thing that stood out to me the most was the old-school rock and roll blaring over the speakers. It struck me that, despite all the finality of death, the atmosphere in the morgue wasn't somber. I guess that was their way of coping, of reminding themselves that it was all in a day's work to discover the cause of someone's demise. I personally couldn't imagine doing that job, but I was enormously appreciative of those who did.

As we watched, the medical examiners would occasionally usher us over to take a closer look at the organs in the bodies they were working on. They took the time to show us what healthy organs looked like versus diseased organs, pointing to where each was located, and then having us watch as they removed it and placed it onto the scale, explaining what this data was telling them about the cause of death. When someone finished one autopsy, they'd go to the large freezers on one side of the large room, open a door, and roll out another steel gurney, already fitted with a ready-to-autopsy body. Rather than being scared or repulsed, I was fascinated.

Well, after we'd seen the process through four times, one of the doctors turned to us, suddenly looking serious. The whole mood of the room changed, as if the air had been let out. He said, "You guys can watch this next autopsy if you want to, but you have to observe it from outside, through the window where you first entered the building." The doctor explained that the deceased was a child, possibly an abuse case. We looked at each other and decided that we would like to observe, so we headed to the window and waited. Moments later, the examiners opened the door of the freezer and wheeled out a small body covered by a sheet. Sure enough, it was a little girl who looked to be about five years old. The cause of death was supposedly an accidental drowning—the story was that she'd fallen getting out of the bathtub, hitting her head on the side. But as the autopsy proceeded, it became apparent to me and everyone else that this little girl had suffered a short, miserable lifetime of abuse. Her skull was covered with bruises, not just the one that would've resulted from hitting her head. I looked through the glass in horror. What caused someone to inflict such harm on anyone, much less a little child? Another cold lesson in life, I guess. That was our last autopsy of the day, and my husband and I spent the hour-and-a-half drive home in silence, caught up in our own thoughts.

Not all of paramedic school was as difficult as that, but none of it was easy. I persisted, though, and in the end, was so glad I did, because it meant I got to join the ranks of some of the most aggressive, assertive, intelligent old-school paramedics in the country. If you ever find yourself in Broward County, calling 911 with a life-threatening emergency, let me assure you that you will be in excellent hands. It was awe-inspiring to me as an EMT to watch and learn from some of these people—and even more so to work alongside them as a fellow paramedic. These folks had watched Johnny Gage and Roy DeSoto on *Emergency!* in the '70s and wanted to emulate them—and they did a damn good job, too. Some went further in their careers and became nurses, nurse practitioners, physician assistants, and even doctors. They were cool as cucumbers on the worst of scenes, and they were happy to pass along valuable information to any of us willing to learn and listen.

Our little department was little no longer—and others had merged with us, so now that I was a paramedic, there were new opportunities I couldn't pass up. It was exhausting to take both the driver-engineer and the lieutenant tests in the same month, but I passed both and chose to jump into the deep end, taking the promotion to lieutenant, which now meant life on a rescue truck—or as the fire guys fondly referred to it, "the Pus Bus."

My first assignment as a newly minted paramedic and lieutenant was at one of our busiest inner-city stations, where I had previously been on the engine. Now, I was on the rescue, and the other person on the truck was brand-new, green as grass. Boy, was he in for quite the initiation (and so was I, for that matter), because during my first shift on the rescue, that young kid and I ran thirty calls in twenty-four hours. The last patient that day had overdosed on crack cocaine. When we arrived, he was handcuffed and lying on his belly outside a run-down gas station. Big mistake. Having a patient lie face down means his bodyweight is compressing his diaphragm and he's liable to become unable to breathe. I yelled to the police officers on scene to turn him over so he wouldn't code, and then the two of us managed to treat him and transport him to the hospital, cops following us. After this call, like any other, the truck had to be decontaminated, restocked, and prepped for the next call. Finally, it was time for shift change and my long drive home.

• • •

People ask me frequently why a fire truck arrives on scene with the rescue truck for a medical call. Our patients are often angry about it, as they don't like the attention a big red fire truck inevitably attracts. Well, in today's multitasking, modern, progressive world, being cross-trained is essential. That means everyone on the fire engine, ladder truck, and tanker is a dual-certified paramedic and firefighter. (I used to joke with civilians that the only difference between the two is that the fire engine could not transport a patient unless they wanted us to throw them on top of the hose bed.)

So why send both? Well, most paramedics ran their asses off with only two people on a truck. This means one paramedic is driving while the officer is in the back of the rig treating the patient, documenting everything for the report, and yelling through the open space at the driver to prep the ER for what we're bringing in and when. (Not to mention the paperwork, which the officer would have to update continuously while treating the patient. This is many paramedics' Achille's heel, but my experience as a secretary helped enormously.) If the patient took a turn for the worst, the driver would have to pull over, and the other medic would jump into the back while the officer called for the engine to respond to a code three! So, you can see why having more folks on hand from the get-go could significantly improve our ability to treat patients efficiently and effectively. When medical calls turned out to be life-threatening, we often needed the full resources of both trucks.

The big red fire trucks are called ALS, "advanced life support," and they carry the same life-saving medical equipment as the rescue truck. This was known as more bang for your buck, and the two professions go hand in hand anyway. These kinds of calls were literally all hands on deck, with both engine and rescue crews working seamlessly together like a well-oiled machine. Airway, breathing, and circulation (the ABCs) always took priority. Then vital signs, IVs, intubation, O2 as necessary, then maybe drug intervention or bandaging, and then packaging the patient for transport via rescue or, with trauma, calling the helicopter for transport. The paramedics on the helicopter were extraordinary, experienced, and always a very welcomed sight. I loved seeing experienced crews work together on serious medical or fire calls, knowing what had to be done, and collaborating to make it happen.

If there were students riding with us on those calls, they got to experience these high-stakes scenarios firsthand, even getting involved, depending on their level of training. If they were only EMTs, or if they were shell-shocked, I would tell them they weren't helping anybody by keeping their hands in your pockets. "Grab a red medical waste bag and put trash into it," I'd say. "And most importantly, do not even think of touching anything without gloves!"

When I became a lieutenant and, later, a captain, I orchestrated the whole scene on these calls, overseeing treatments and relaying important information to incoming crews, the chief, and the hospital. Especially if trauma was involved, they needed to know quickly so they were ready and waiting, either outside or up on the roof at the helipad. It is an incredible, coordinated effort between agencies to save lives, and I was humbled to be a part of it.

•••

After that first inner-city stint, I was awarded a bid as a lieutenant on a rescue truck in an affluent area just on the edge of the Everglades. The city paid the county for an extra paramedic on their trucks, and that made running calls a lot easier, because most of the time, it meant the engine didn't need to respond for added manpower.

This station bid was considered one of the best because it was newer and in a nice neighborhood, and it wasn't usually crazy busy like the urban areas tend to be. The lower call volume meant the crews could eat dinner together and sleep most of the night in our community bunkroom, which we called "Gen Pop." It was a fairly large room with rows of twin beds down each side. We each bought our own sheets, blankets, and pillows because the standard-issue ones were awful. Once I had pink polka dot sheets, but my favorite color was cobalt blue. Others, guys included, stole their kids' Cinderella, cartoon hero, or monster sheets. We wore crocs around the station for comfort, and mine were blue with miniature fire and rescue trucks and Maltese cross pins attached through the holes.

Our beds were separated by lockers and blackout curtains (which we'd designed and paid for ourselves), and most everyone bought their own fans to block out the noises and the smells, but we'd still laugh and talk to each other from our separate little spaces. You learned to sleep with lights and TVs and the sounds and smells of farts wafting through the room (and the subsequent laughter from the guys, who turned into twelve-year-old boys). You also learned to perk up to listen to a call coming over the radio, then go back to sleep if it wasn't for your crew.

I enjoyed the camaraderie, but I relished having my own room when possible as an officer. I'd lie in bed with my jumpsuit on, zipped up to the waist over my T-shirt so I just had to pull it up, put my arms through the sleeves, zip, and go to respond to a call, and I always slept with my socks on to save time. (There was a time when we kept bunker boots and pants by our beds so we could quickly get dressed when needed. Later, though, this was determined to be a health hazard, given the cancer-causing chemicals that permeated most of our gear. So outside those went.)

Another perk of this station was that the citizens of the surrounding community would drop off cakes and cookies, drawings their kids had made, or letters they'd written thanking us, and we gladly showed them the trucks whenever they asked. The sheer delight on little kids' faces when we lifted them up into the driver's seat of the big red truck, letting them blow the air horns and sirens, was priceless. I got to know the sons and daughters of some of the men and women I worked with, too. It was fun to see them as kids coming around to visit Daddy or Mommy at the station and then watch them grow up, some eventually becoming officers and colleagues. It must've been in their blood.

There were lots of reasons to love this station, but I didn't let its quiet nature lull me into complacency. As I've said, you never know what you are going to respond to when the tones go off.

SIXTEEN

THIS IS YOUR CAPTAIN SPEAKING

Unfortunately, I wouldn't get to stick around that idyllic station in the Everglades long, because I still had work to do. Not long into my career, I'd known that I wanted to become an officer, and now that I was a lieutenant, I was angling for captain.

Was it presumption, bravado, arrogance, or confidence? Maybe a bit of all of those things. Fortunately, the glass ceiling is not prevalent in the fire service. I got paid the same amount as men, and that pay was based on my rank, education, time on the job, and union representation. In short, there was plenty of opportunity for me to climb that career ladder if I wanted to.

I was driven to excel, and I learned by emulating the best traits of officers—male or female—that I would have gone to hell and back with. And I also learned plenty from leaders whose example I decidedly *did not* want to follow. I participated in plenty of calls where I felt the officer made terrible decisions, sometimes scaring the hell out of me. I was lucky to not get myself seriously hurt but knew I didn't want to be under the command of people like this forever. It doesn't serve anybody well to become a Monday morning quarterback, but watching these leaders make decisions I disagreed with made me think about how I would handle things once I was in charge.

As I watched other leaders—the good, the bad, and the ugly—and worked toward my own ascent up the chain of officers, I developed three leadership rules that I pledged to follow throughout the rest of my career.

My first leadership rule was never to scream at or belittle some-one on scene, but I did vow to lead with authority. If it was a safety issue and lives were at stake, then I would have to be harsh to keep things going our way when time was of the essence. Otherwise, I strove to remember that making mistakes is part of learning, and humiliation is the opposite of inspiration. I learned this the hard way when I was still riding backward on an engine as the rookie firefighter-EMT, perfecting my new medical skills during a response to a minor school bus accident. I was applying a head bed to immo-bilize a patient who was on the stretcher, preparing for transport. I didn't get it taped properly, but rather than calmly correcting me, the paramedic on scene screamed at me in front of everyone.

This particular paramedic, a female, had a reputation for being disrespectful to her female colleagues. She was charming with the males in the station, but she ignored (at best) most other females in the firehouse. I never understood why. Maybe it was just her insecurity. She was certainly knowledgeable, but her toxic attitude turned me off completely.

Having come of age in the '70s, I was well aware of tyrant female bosses. It was a time when women seemed to resent other women getting promoted—or sharing the spotlight in any way. I have seen many positive changes over the years, but recent events, such as the terrible partial collapse of the Champlain Towers South in Surfside, have given me pause. A good friend of mine, a female battalion chief, was on the urban search-and-rescue crew responding to that tragedy. This extraordinary young woman started as a probie and had progressed to the rank of battalion chief in a relatively short period of time. When the incident occurred, she responded within the hour, bringing her beloved search-and-rescue dog out of retirement. She and her dog, along with the other members of the crew, worked long hours around the clock, without a break, to find possible survivors.

The worldwide news coverage of this tragedy was a constant, and the media noticed my friend and her dog, featuring her in a couple of firefighting trade publications. Social media exploded with commentary, of course, and while most of it was positive, the volume of very negative comments from other females made me wonder if we have truly come far enough to respect and support one another like we should. They questioned her frequent presence in photographs and articles, accusing her of deliberately seeking fame. These reactions were appalling. I understand what it is like to be a rare female in this industry and to be an officer profiled while working a scene. Let me assure you: If you're just seeking fame, there are much easier ways to go about it.

Anyway, many years after I got screamed at as a rookie, when I was a new captain floating all over the county, I had the good fortune to work with newly hired people and put my "no embarrassing my crew" rule into practice. There was a list of chore assignments at each station, to be completed after dinner. One night, I noticed a young man looking at the chart with a funny look on his face. When I saw he'd been assigned to clean the bathrooms, I could've started laying into him right then and there about what he was waiting for and why he hadn't gotten to work. But that wasn't my style. Instead,

I pulled him aside so as not to embarrass him and asked if he had any questions. He told me rather sheepishly that he didn't know how to clean a bathroom, because his mother had always taken care of it at home.

Many a captain would have "educated" this young man by embarrassing him in front of his fellow new hires. But again, not my style. Instead, I said, "Well, come with me, young man, and I will show you how to clean the bathroom so thoroughly, you'll impress any officer in any station." First, I told him to put on gloves and grab the toilet brush and cleaner. "Pour the cleaner into each toilet bowl, and brush the inside," I instructed him. "But don't flush it. That way, the next person to use it can see the blue liquid, confirming it was cleaned." I grabbed the can of Lysol and sprayed it around the rim and the bottom and top of each toilet seat. Next, I told him to always make sure the toilet paper holder was full, and I showed him how to replace the current roll and fill up the storage space with extra paper towels and toilet paper. Next, I told him to wipe the mirrors and empty the trash bags, leaving a couple of extras in each can. Then, we walked through the last steps: Sweep and mop the floor, and *voila!* Done. I know cleaning a bathroom sounds simple to most people, but if you've never done it before, well, how would you know?

It's the little things we're not taught in fire school that can make a difference in how we lead. It made me proud that this young man was brave enough to ask me how to clean a bathroom. I ran into him a few months later at another station, and he pulled me aside to thank me profusely for teaching him instead of embarrassing him that day.

My second leadership rule was less warm and fuzzy: Never cut corners. When I was in paramedic school, I encountered plenty of paramedics who were just lazy, encouraging patients to refuse transport just to alleviate their workload. It was shameful, and I wouldn't stand for it. Yes, I was accused of being a pain-in-the-ass officer, but I didn't care. Each patient was somebody's mother father, child, brother, or sister, and deserved to be treated—if nothing else, for the sake of their loved ones. That was my philosophy, and I expected nothing less from my crews.

And my third and favorite rule: In the fire station, we're family. Don't get me wrong: I demanded the best from the crews I worked with, and I didn't put up with negligence, disrespect, or bad attitudes. But it was important for me, as a leader in these firehouses, to take care of my crews.

Many of the guys were gorgeous, young, and single, and I felt like a mama bear. I listened to their woes—mostly about girlfriends, many of whom were pressuring my guys for a ring. Since I was older, I had witnessed the fallout when people married too soon and quickly discovered the idyllic life they'd envisioned was not reality. I always encouraged them to talk with their partners about expectations. Would she work or stay home and raise the kids? Did she like her job, or was she going to quit the minute they married? Was she in school, studying for a career?

I also cautioned them to be sure their partners were in it for the long haul and not just the "glamor" of dating a firefighter. After all, there is a kind of "hero worship" aspect to attraction, and some folks—male and female—just want to hook up with a firefighter, not realizing what that really entails. (Fortunately, I never had to deal with those kinds of problems, because I met my future husband on the job. He knew how driven and dedicated I was to this career, and he was proud of me—and visa-versa.) I am not judging the people who are just attracted to the *idea* of being with a firefighter, but I've seen the potential bad outcomes firsthand, and when you get right down to it, I didn't want the young guys in my command to get their hearts broken. We were a family, and if they asked me for advice, I would gladly give it to them.

I told them they were like golden geese—young, handsome, with a great career that paid well, including benefits and plenty of time off. But once you added marriage and kids into that mix, it would be a whole different game. Marriage means committing to another job—as spouse and possibly parent—after your shift at the station. That is fine if that is what you and your partner both decide, but it's important not to take that commitment lightly, and to be sure the person you decide to make it with is as committed as you are.

This is, frankly, true no matter what industry you're in, how old you are, or what gender you are. But being a leader in a predominantly male profession, the stories I'd heard and witnessed were mostly centered around my male colleagues who were hurting in miserable marriages because they would rather stay in it for the kids or because it was "cheaper to keep her." Their pensions could suffer if they divorced, and I guess they would rather stay in than lose everything they had worked for. I got to see the other side of that coin up close and personal with my own father, of course, so I didn't have a whole lot of sympathy for some of those guys. They'd made their beds. But still, many of the young guys on my crew had time to avoid those mistakes.

Don't get me wrong: I wasn't advising the boys against marriage—I was all for it if they knew they'd found the right person and that's what they both wanted. For example, one of the guys I worked with frequently was involved with two women and bemoaning the fact that he couldn't decide which one he preferred. Well, I told him when he just wanted to breathe the same air as the woman he was with, he would know she was the one. Funny thing: He took my advice and married the one. They had a couple of kids, he eventually retired, and they are still happily married.

As much as I enjoyed getting to know my people, hearing about their personal lives, and sharing advice when I could, I was proudest of them—and of my own leadership—when my crews did a good job on calls, not only addressing the emergency but taking the best care of our callers that they could. One particular non-emergency visit to a brand-new independent living facility for people fifty-five and older stands out as a prime example.

We responded to many calls in nursing homes, and let me just say, most of them are not where you want to end up, but sometimes it is necessary. My own mother suffered from Alzheimer's and had a tendency to wander, telling my brother before she left the house that she was "going home." The last time she did it, the local police had to find her, and she was put into a nursing home where she spent the last year and a half of her life. It was heartbreaking, to say the least, but I challenge anyone who says they would never put their mother or father in a place like that to try and manage their care at home before being so judgmental.

Anyway, this complex—an independent living facility—was far from the depressing picture of a "nursing home" that many of us have in our heads. There were several floors of condos, sixteen individual villas, an on-site restaurant, game room, dance hall, bar, pool, and hot tub. There were numerous social activities for the residents, and the staffed nurse's station was staffed twenty-four-seven. The floors were Italian marble, and the décor was upscale. Most of the residents were in their seventies and older but still active, not yet in need of extensive care. It seemed like a nice place to live if you could afford it.

Once the building was occupied, we arranged an informal meeting in the large conference room along with the fire marshal, manager, security personnel, and various staff of the building to answer questions and listen to suggestions or concerns from the new residents. It is important that first responders get to know people in the community where they serve and create a professional relationship, and we thought this was particularly true for the seniors who would feel more comfortable dialing 911 if they knew a familiar face would respond. (Dialing 911 can be scary for anyone, but especially so for elderly patients.) In this friendly context, the elderly men's and women's eyes lit up when they saw us, and they wasted no time in asking us questions about ourselves. On my truck that day was a rookie named David. He was very attractive, and the old ladies really took a shine to him. The other guys and I just laughed, teased him a little bit, and continued our conversations with the residents.

Usually, we try to stay together as a group, but when we finished, we realized David had disappeared into the large crowd of residents. I knew he had a radio on him so we could find him if he got into trouble, but there was no need. He reappeared shortly and said he just got caught up talking to the women, no harm done. I was proud of him that day—he'd made a sincere effort to get to know his community and his potential patients, and I thought he handled himself quite admirably in a situation that would've made many guys his age uncomfortable. It was moments like that that made me proud to be an officer and proud of the leadership philosophies I'd developed and was passing on to my crews.

• • •

Of course, moving up the ranks meant being okay with sacrificing some of the comforts my years of hard work and dedication had earned me. For example, after a couple of years at that cushy station out west in the Everglades, I took a bid on another rescue on the east side of town. This station was so busy, they sometimes ran two rescues in order to handle the extreme call volume. Everybody thought I had lost my mind—I was now considered an old-timer, and I didn't have to prove anything anymore, so they couldn't understand why I'd choose a more difficult job. I knew all that, but I gave up my golden bid anyway. I wanted to be promoted to captain, and I knew that sharpening my skills and getting to know people in this other station—rather than resting on my laurels in my previous, prized bid—would help me do just that.

I was elated to have a change of scenery and excited about my new assignment. I pulled into the new station on my first day and proceeded to haul in all of my stuff, making several trips. I had my bedding, my extra uniforms, my jumpsuits, and my dress uniform just in case something official came up in a hurry. I also had a small igloo cooler with food and snacks, my bunker gear, and a duffle bag full books, magazines, and training manuals. And, of course, I had my workout gear and towels. I looked like a bag lady carrying in boatloads of stuff, preparing for Armageddon.

This station was old, composed of a main office, a day room, a kitchen, and personnel offices upfront, with gen pop and a tiny officers' quarters in the back. But behind the front office, there was another small bedroom specifically for the EMS officers. When I walked in, one of the two twin beds was made up with sheets, a blanket, and a pillow, and the other had personal stuff on it. Clearly, someone had already taken up residence. Since I was the new officer on the rescue, though, it seemed fitting that this would be my room, so I walked out into the front room and asked the guys just who was occupying that space. Once they told me who it was—and confirmed he was not assigned to the rescue truck—I said boldly, "There's a new sheriff in town. I am the EMS lieutenant, and that is now my room."

Eyes opened wide, and jaws dropped.

I knew the guy who had been using that room, and I liked him, but he was a driver on the ladder truck and had no business bunking there. In fact, he'd been relegated to the rescue room because nobody could stand his snoring, and they begged me not to put him back in gen pop with the rest of the crew. But I didn't flinch. I stood my ground. "I don't care," I said. "He just needs a C-Pap machine like 99 percent of the people on this job."

At that, he piped up. "I have one," he said, "but it's so uncomfortable, I hate to wear it." I told him to get used to it, because this was my room.

In hindsight, I guess I should have handled things differently (leadership rule number one, and all), but I didn't. The regular captain was off that day, but he later told me that his phone blew up shortly after my arrival!

"Who the fuck does she think she is coming in here saying there's a new sheriff in town?" they asked. And, "Where does she get off kicking him out of that room?" And, "We can't have him in gen pop! He snores like a damn freight train! We'll never get any rest."

The complaints went on and on, but the fact was that I was right. The captain calmly told them I was the new rescue lieutenant, and since that room was for EMS personnel, I had every right to kick him out and claim it for my own. The snorer got fitted for a more comfortable C-Pap machine and slept in gen pop.

Fortunately, we remained friends. Because in my new bid, friends would be more important than ever. This new-to-me station in this little city that had merged with Broward Fire-Rescue would turn out to be one of the craziest places I have ever worked. The area's nickname was "City of the Trees" because it was full of beautiful old trees, and some of the developments would trick you into thinking it was Mayberry. Well, it was more like the Twilight Zone. We ran terrible car accidents and plenty of fires, but more often than not, our calls were for drug overdoses. It seemed like everybody was overdosing on something in that little town—mostly oxycodone or bath salts. The rehab facility across the street from the station kept us running. They had a temporary holding area where minor females were housed in cells that looked more like cages until the state could decide what to do with them. And, I learned, when people with good insurance would fly in to start rehab, they often liked to have their last hurrah before beginning their detox. We would frequently transport these insurance rich middle-class folks to the hospital so they could be checked out before starting rehab.

So where did all these overdoses come from? Pill mills were highly prevalent in Broward County at the time—in fact, we had the unfortunate distinction of being at the heart of that particular boom—and the addicted residents were savvy enough to obtain pictures of back injuries on the internet, make them look like theirs, and pay cash for prescription pain medications by the bottles. How do I know this? A drug addict told me. He was so young, and he told me he'd lost more than a dozen friends to overdoses, mostly from oxy that came from these terrible places.

Needless to say, it was a busy house—so busy that there were two rescues with three people on each, in addition to an engine and a ladder truck. I worked on all of them and learned a lot about leadership from the captain. He was a few years younger than me, and he had a reputation for being a hard ass, but I had a good, solid relationship with him, and he always had my back. Under his watchful eye, I learned to delegate and orchestrate when on scene, stepping back from my hands-on approach as a firefighter-paramedic and into officer mode. Now, that doesn't mean doing nothing, especially if there is a shortage of people on scene, but it does mean embracing a different mindset. As the lieutenant, I gave the orders and documented the treatment from arrival on scene to the arrival at the hospital.

Another important lesson I learned while working out of that station was that "Control + Z" will bring back information you've lost on your computer. This lesson came not from the captain but from an overdosed young guy we were treating. I was frustrated with the new reporting system and the portable Toughbook laptop we were now using to record patient information and document calls. While I was typing en route to the hospital, we hit a bump in the road, and I accidentally deleted all the information the patient had given me.

"Damn this computer," I said to my partner who was treating him in the back of the rescue. "I just lost everything."

"Control Z," the young, drug-overdose patient said nonchalantly.

"What?" I was sitting in the chair directly behind the stretcher and his head.

"Hit control and Z at the same time," he repeated. I did, and like magic, the lost information reappeared.

"Just because I'm a drug addict doesn't mean I'm stupid," he said smugly. "I know computers."

Well, what do you know?

Despite how busy the station was, I did manage to study while I was on the job, and after twenty-three years of service, I finally got promoted to captain in 2010! As far as captains go, my new status meant I was at the bottom of the rank and would have to start floating from station to station again. But that was okay. I was ready to get out of this place, and I liked floating. Even before I became a captain, I'd floated into stations 90 percent of my career, mostly by choice. It was my way of keeping fresh and preventing boredom. I loved working on different trucks—one shift on the ladder truck, then another on an engine, tanker, or rescue. They all fulfilled me in different ways.

Being the captain would mean I was responsible for all the crews on all the different trucks in whatever station I floated into. Usually, though, I would be back on an engine or a ladder truck, which was always my first love.

That said, floating wasn't all roses. If you had the crew from hell, a twenty-four-hour shift could seem like a week. (And as captain, it often meant adding extra shifts. Once, I worked five forty-eight-hour shifts in a row for a great female captain who wanted to drive out west for a long vacation with her family. Let's just say I wouldn't do that again—or at least, not for just anybody.)

It was also a major pain in the ass to schlep all my stuff around. And it wasn't just the stuff I needed for my shift, either; we were supposed to be prepared to stay at a station for up to a week in case of disaster. For example, when a storm became a hurricane and a warning was issued, we were supposed to get our homes and family members safe and secure and report for duty. When Hurricane Andrew was headed for South Florida in 1992, my husband and I were called in on a Sunday afternoon. It was quite an eerie sight, just the two of us lonely travelers headed south on the turnpike while northbound was bumper-to-bumper with evacuees. I had packed three-ounce pop-top cans of tuna and a bunch of little kids' cereal boxes, and when I got to the station, I threw them into a compartment on the engine. Fifty-two back-to-back calls later, the crew was very happy I had thought to do that. With no downtime for proper meals between calls, we were starving!

Making my way up through the ranks to captain wasn't easy, but I'm proud of the leader I became, and I would do it over and over again. Firefighters and paramedics are trained to respond to emergency situations and stay calm even during the most chaotic scenes, but you can't train someone to have empathy and a desire to serve. It must come from within your heart and soul. I knew I had those key qualities in spades, but I honestly didn't know that I could be so strong, that I could handle leading a crew of men and women into potential danger, or that I could take charge during life-saving medical situations. But I did it. I learned to have confidence in myself, my crew, my training, and experience. I even like to think I developed a little wisdom over time. Yes, I still made mistakes, and no, I didn't always handle difficult crew members according to my own leadership rules. Sure, if I had to do it over knowing what I know now, I would handle some things differently. But that is the universal quandary of life, isn't it?

SEVENTEEN

PAYING IT FORWARD: SHARING MY STORY

While responding to an auto accident in a busy intersection of town one evening, I noticed two elderly women sitting on a bench waiting for the bus, both staring quite intensely at me. I was now a bona fide captain. I was still floating, but most of the time, I was back on an engine or ladder truck. That felt like home to me, and I much preferred that to being on a rescue. I was in full bunker gear, directing my crew. One crew member was doing patient care, the other was pulling a hose line for safety, and I was assisting and talking on the radio. As we finished up, I looked over to see the ladies were still sitting on the bench, staring at me.

I took off my bunker coat and helmet, placing them on the officer seat of the engine, and walked over to them. I smiled, held out my hand to shake theirs, and said, "Hello, how are you ladies doing today?"

They both started talking at once, very animated, telling me how they had watched me and were so proud of me and amazed at how confident and professional I looked. They told me they had both wanted to become firefighters so badly, but it wasn't possible in their day. Women just didn't do that back then. They had limited choices: teacher, nurse, homemaker, secretary, bank teller, or waitress. All of those are important professions, but they're not a lot of options. Women weren't permitted to become firefighters or police officers, because only men could have those careers.

I told them how glad I was that times had changed and how I was proud to be a firefighter and never took it for granted that I was a pioneer. I hoped I could be an inspiration to other women or little girls to consider the fire service.

I walked back to the engine, hopped up into the officer's seat, smiled at them, and waved goodbye before I grabbed the mic. "Engine 66 available."

I enjoyed interacting with the public throughout my career, and most fire-rescue people feel the same way. Moments like that, meeting those two ladies and seeing the joy in their eyes as they witnessed a woman doing a job women in their generation never would've dreamed of was incredibly rewarding. Equally rewarding, however—and a real joy for many of us—was getting to interact with the children in our communities. One of the stations I worked at was near an elementary school, and we loved to see the children walk by on their way to school each morning.

One day, a teacher told us the kids had won a reading competition, so we all stood outside of the station and clapped for them as they walked by. And we got to interact with them at school frequently too. We once read stories to a group of kindergarteners, and we made annual visits during fire prevention week and career week to share our stories with them and tell them all about our jobs.

During these visits, I was always the person who would come into the room all bunkered out with an air pack and my face mask on, with a Nomex hood protecting my head and breathing loudly so they would learn not to be afraid of the firefighters if they were ever trapped in their house during a fire. Then I would methodically take everything off, and when they realized I was a woman, they would gasp. It was priceless.

We'd tailor our presentations depending on the age of the children, of course, going into more detail about all of the equipment on the fire truck for some groups than others. The teenagers usually looked bored with us (though that default boredom made the occasional glimpse of excitement or inspiration even more satisfying), but the little kids would ask question after question after question and tell dozens of (long, drawn-out, and very sweet) stories.

But whether my audience was kindergarteners, middle schoolers, or high schoolers, I was the one they asked about the most. Their curiosity about what it was like to be a girl firefighter warmed my heart, and I hoped to inspire them. I would tell them they could become firefighters, too, and I would laugh at the little boys who would say girls can't be firefighters. I would quickly say, "Oh, yes, they can. If you stay in school, don't get into trouble, eat right, and exercise to stay strong, anyone can be a firefighter." Sometimes the little girls would grab onto me and wrap their little arms around me in all of my bunker gear, squealing and sometimes even crying. This was one of the best aspects of my job: to be able to show them what was possible if they worked hard. One of the most rewarding experiences of my life as a career firefighter-paramedic was talking and teaching, and maybe just perhaps imparting some wisdom to the young people I encountered along the way. This included, as you know by now, the trainees and rookies that came through the stations I worked at. They were so green and wide-eyed, and I appreciated how hard they were trying to appear confident when I knew what they were really feeling, because I had been there, too. I was lucky in the beginning of my career to be taught by good, solid men who made sure that nothing would harm me while I was learning the ropes, and I wanted to pay it forward. They pushed me to grab that nozzle and taught me to always check every piece of equipment on the truck—and remember where it was located. If the officer called for a tool, I knew exactly where it was without question.

My first lieutenant was a little rough around the edges, but he had a big heart of gold. He taught me a lot, and sometimes he had more confidence in my abilities than I did. He insisted the station, truck, and all of the equipment be kept clean and in top condition, and he didn't care if it was late at night or not. I learned from him, and I maintained the same standards once I was in his position. I would remind the probie or rookie who was washing the trucks to scrub the wheel wells and wipe the bottom edge of the compartments when cleaning the roll-up doors. I had appreciated being told these little golden nuggets along the way, and it was important to pass them along.

I was also fortunate to work for leaders who cared about my safety and well-being as much as my performance, and I tried to pay that forward, too. One of the vehicles I learned to drive when I was a green firefighter was an air truck used for filling firefighter bottles on structure fires or hazardous scenes wherever air was needed. I admit that it was scary to drive that truck into dangerous neighborhoods after midnight by myself. There was no GPS at the time—only a radio—so I would look at the map and get an idea of where I was going, and as I got closer to the scene, I would look for the smoke or flashing lights to guide me the rest of the way. After returning to the station, I would park the air truck out on the ramp and refill the system for the next call. My favorite battalion chief would wait up for me on those late nights, keeping his light on and keeping an eye out for me, making sure I was ok outside in front of the station filling the banks of the air truck no matter how late. Once I finished and was backing the truck into the bay and the closed the door, he would go to bed.

I've shared dozens of similar experiences already, and I could share dozens more. But what it comes down to is that I worked with a lot of people who genuinely cared, had a tremendous work ethic, and wanted me to succeed. I hope that I made a positive impact on the young people I worked with, just like these guys did on me. And I hope that, in turn, those young people will pass it on to others in the future.

THE END OF THE BEGINNING, Part 2: I'M REALLY GOING TO LIKE THIS JOB

I looked out one last time at the uniformed personnel, who had been standing in rows respectfully for over an hour now. Seeing the rows of men and women I'd had the pleasure to work with, some on their very first days, made me smile. I wondered how their stories would turn out, and I silently wished them much success.

And then I glanced over in the opposite direction, at my husband, my nephew, my friends, and the retirees that had taken the time to show up to bid me farewell.

As the Honor Guard, The Black Pearl Pipes and Drums Band, and the chief prepared to parade out, ending the ceremony, I thought back to that first day on shift, nearly thirty years before.

First of all, that day, I was still processing the fact that I had made it through a very tough process, physically and mentally. From making it through fire academy to enduring over five weeks of boot camp with ten other wonderful souls who had started this journey with me, the months leading up to this day felt like a dream. Then, to be welcomed by a stellar crew of guys into my new fire family proved to me that I had finally found what I had been searching for my whole life:

A calling, a future, and best of all, home.

I remembered sitting on the couch in the dayroom on that first shift. The guys were throwing around a NERF ball in gym shorts and no shirts, and they paid no mind to me staring at them. I was just another part of their crew—their family. I'd been welcomed as a sister in their brotherhood.

God, I thought to myself, *I am really going to like this job.*

LIFE AFTER THE
BAY DOOR CLOSES

Over the years, many people have asked me about my career and my experiences as a firefighter-paramedic. Not surprisingly, a common question is, "What's the worst call you ever responded to?" First, there were too many to choose just one. Second, I tried not to elaborate too much on any of the tough calls, because the things my crew and I witnessed are the stuff of nightmares for most people. Instead, I decided to write a book about my experiences—including some of those terrible calls, but also sharing a more well-rounded look at what my career entailed and, more importantly, what it meant to me. That, of course, is the book you've just read. Now, I want to take you behind the scenes of the first months of my retirement to show you exactly how this book came about.

My years on the job were thrilling, terrifying, funny, sad, dangerous, and yes, sometimes boring. But they were never ordinary. After my retirement, I never expected to miss the adrenaline rush so much. I thought I was ready to put it all behind me—the uncertainty of each call, the pressure of knowing my job was to help our citizens get through the worst day of their lives, doing our best to make a positive difference. It takes skill, experience, gut feeling, training, cooperation with crew members, and sometimes just good, old common sense to do that. It takes developing detective-like instincts to sort out the chaos of an emergency scene. You also need to stay focused and be able to give orders, to listen to what has happened, timestamp and document everything, render treatment if necessary, and prioritize what needs to be done first, whether you're dealing with a fire, car accident, hazmat incident, or domestic abuse call. You need to know your department's protocols and standard operating procedures and follow them.

This was the life I had worked so hard for. I had cherished every minute of it, but it hadn't been easy, and as I stood on that stage during my ceremony, I was confident I was ready to leave it behind. Besides, I was (and still am) so grateful to have been able to retire healthy alongside the man I love, who also was able to retire healthy. However, shortly afterward, I was faced with a shocking reality. Rather than allowing me to relax like I'd always imagined, retirement kicked me into an abyss of depression and uncertainty. My confidence was shredded, and I fought weight gain and anxiety.

The discipline of the fire service had been such an important part of my life for so long—from preparing my uniform for shift the next day to loading my car the night before with all my stuff. Yes, I should have bought stock in Niagara Falls spray starch, but I had always felt a sense of pride, routine, and comfort when ironing my uniform and polishing my boots and belt.

I had felt like a part of the crew when the guys at my first station taught me how to properly shine my boots. All of the firehouses had a wooden box of shoe polish, cloths, and an assortment of brushes to use, but the key to getting shiny boots is good, old-fashioned spit. That's right. First, you apply the polish with a brush or cloth, then you gather up a big old mouthful of spit and let it rip onto the top of the boot. Then, you brush them for a guaranteed glossy shine. Repeat regularly to keep looking your best.

This was all part of my routine, and when it was over, I had no structure. It has taken me a few years to truly appreciate the freedom of staying up late and reading my Kindle at 3:00 a.m. without worrying about the alarm going off at 4:30 a.m. for my long drive to work. More importantly, it took me a while to embrace the freedom of spending time with my husband, traveling, and celebrating holidays together—which we had rarely been able to do before—and appreciating the fact that we are still together, happy, and healthy.

Yes, it was much more difficult than I had ever imagined to leave this career that had meant so much to me—that had given me my first experience of stability, of putting down roots. People, including myself, relish the "countdown to retirement," but what I learned is that retirement may not be as perfect as we imagine. I needed *something* to give me a renewed sense of purpose, and for me, through the depression and recovery, writing became that something. I had always enjoyed it, but during that terrible season of my life, my passion for writing became serious, and it pulled me out of the depths.

Because I know I'm not alone in this experience, I wanted to share here some of the writing that helped me process just how distraught I was—and helped me rebuild that confident, purpose-filled foundation. These pieces are full of raw emotion, only lightly edited. In them, you'll see some stories and ideas you've already encountered in these pages, and that's no coincidence. In my effort and desire to mentor young females who are interested in the

Fire-Rescue service, I started a blog called *Sister In A Brotherhood*. It was my sincere attempt to reach out to females and start a candid conversation about my experiences and perhaps theirs as well. Eventually, I elected to stop blogging in favor of writing a book. This book. The essays that follow—some of them posts from the original blog—were the spark that led to the book you hold in your hands. I hope that, by sharing them here, I'll be able to help someone else out there who has retired and is suffering. The following essay was written in the fall of 2015.

WHAT DO YOU MEAN I'M NOT BULLETPROOF!

I could have sworn that I was wearing a blue shirt with a giant "S" on it, invisible cape billowing behind me.

I had been a fearless, strong, female firefighter-paramedic for almost thirty years. I'd worked for a very diverse, busy, urban department, and my motto was to always do the right thing by the people you work with and the citizens you serve, especially those whose lives depend on us.

Tragedy happened to other people, not me.

Yes, I had lost both of my parents, my only brother, countless friends, and beloved animals. But nothing could prepare me for what these last two years of my life—including my first few months of retirement—would bring.

Who knew that a furry German Shepherd puppy, with big paws and razor teeth, whom we'd lovingly named Timber, would be the precipice to plunge me into a great big black hole with his untimely passing. I never imagined the sheer physical and mental pain his death—two years ago, on Earth Day 2014—would cause me. Maybe I should be embarrassed or ashamed by my grief, but even as I express my darkest thoughts, two years later, the sunlight is finally starting to appear once again.

I vividly remember coming home after a horrific shift shortly after losing him. I hated the quiet and emptiness of my house. Exhausted and brokenhearted, I just grabbed his toys and the lock of fur we'd saved, and I crumbled into a ball, sobbing in a corner of my house. The emptiness in my heart—the utter sadness of coming home to a quiet house without that furry face greeting me with barks of sheer joy that Mama was home—was excruciating. There were times when I thought I would rather be with Timber than continue living life with my wonderful husband. Though he was grieving too, he knew that life goes on, and so should we.

Well, after many long, dark days running on autopilot, I could see retirement coming. In a way, I was thankful, because I was working in the station from hell and the only way out was to start floating again, which would mean living out of my car every shift. But still, I was dreading leaving the structured, stable way of life that I came to depend on.

Flash forward to the ceremony.

It was everything I had hoped it would be and more. Friends and family were in attendance, along with colleagues, various chiefs, and even the mayor—all paying respect and tributes to my almost-thirty-year career. Afterward, my husband and I threw a bang-up retirement party at his golf club, replete with delicious food, an open bar, and great music for our closest friends in a beautiful setting on the St. Lucie River.

What was not to be ecstatic about?

Still, there was a black hole in my heart, now filled with uncertainty as I faced an impending cross-country move. It was meant to be a new chapter in our lives in a completely new environment, a new, exciting adventure, and maybe for some people, it would have been.

But not for me.

I felt uprooted and depressed. Slowly but surely, my downward spiral began. I know they say home is where the heart is and should be wherever you are with the one you love. But still, the blue suit with the flowing cape and the giant "S" on the front was beginning to disintegrate right before my eyes.

I had lost my shield and my armor.

I became fearful of nearly everything. I refused to drive in my temporary new home, and I hated coming back to it even though it was filled with loving, generous friends who tried desperately to help me dig myself out of the dark hole I was in.

My husband told me later that he almost had me committed; he couldn't even recognize the person I had become. Where was his strong, beautiful, fierce, bright light of a wife? If he was anything less than a saint, he would have pulled up his stakes and fled for the hills.

But he didn't.

In hindsight, I don't know how he got through it himself, worrying about me, trying to break through any way he thought might work, sometimes speaking to me softly, and sometimes harshly; neither method worked.

We are different people. He walked away from the fire service with a sterling career and an even more impressive record, having enlisted in the Coast Guard at age eighteen before becoming a firefighter. When he retired, he said, "I have given my all to being a civil servant, and now it's time for me, and us!" Desperate as I was, I couldn't find that same spirit for a long time.

Then, after a cruise to Alaska last year—our retirement present to ourselves, to celebrate our accomplishments and toast our bright future—I started to get sick. I had been feeling so exhausted most of the time, and I just couldn't shake it no matter how hard I'd tried to immerse myself in the new adventures during the numerous weekend trips my husband had planned only for our enjoyment.

But after Alaska, it really wiped me out. First, the genuine, kick-you-in-the-ass flu, then an abscessed tooth that made me want to saw my face off. It seemed to be a downward spiral but thank goodness our return home to Florida was in sight. Surely then my blue shirt with the giant "S" and the invisible flowing cape would reappear.

But, no, it didn't.

I was happy to finally be back home in my house, in my comfort zone, with my friends all around. But still, that void where my furry boy Timber had once been clouded everything, along with the looming decisions of what our future would hold for us—together or apart—which really compounded my sadness.

Then, another bout of respiratory infection reared its ugly head again.

To be perfectly honest, I imagine the excessive drinking, eating, and traveling didn't help as I tried to chase away my funk. "Cry me a river, you say," but this is my story, and by peeling back the not-so-pretty layers, I hope I can finally heal, and I hope I just might help you, too.

After not one but two more bouts of respiratory infections, in addition to the shoulder surgery I have scheduled for next week, I have finally surrendered my blue shirt with the giant "S," along with the flowing, invisible cape.

For now.

Lying in bed for a week gives you time for reflection.

Not only have I discovered that there's strength in allowing myself to be still, rest, and just breathe, but I am also finally thinking about and embracing a new future. I'm healthy, happy, and willing to allow new experiences to lift me up instead of plunging me back into darkness.

As I lie here looking out into my beautiful green yard filled with palm trees, I give thanks. Glancing around my bedroom, filled with memories of that big, furry boy jumping on my bed, licking my face, wagging his tail, and plopping down beside me, I give thanks again.

The tears are flowing, and they will probably continue from time to time, as Timber was so special to me, but the time has come to say goodbye to him for now, allowing him to go back to the coveted place in my heart where he will always remain.

It's time to stop the sadness and let the physical and mental healing begin. It won't happen overnight, but that's okay. I will not push it away or expect it to disappear. Instead, I will concentrate on what's truly important to me in this life:

My priceless husband, whose strength I have tried to push away instead of embracing. I can always trust him to have my best interests at heart even though we sometimes have to agree to disagree. We will always find our way to the next chapter.

My many friends who are there for me—and I for them—no matter what the geographical distance might be.

And last but certainly not least, my sister Linda, who has always been there for me. She listens to my deepest thoughts, my worst fears, and my craziest ideas, as I do hers. Sometimes we laugh, sometimes we cry, and sometimes we just think we are batshit crazy.

Hey, wait a minute.

I think I see a glimpse of that blue shirt with the giant "S" on the front, and the flowing invisible cape behind.

We shall see.

Fast Forward; 2019

PICKING AT SCABS

It is an honor and a privilege to be able to retire healthy and happy, enjoying time with friends and family. But it is quite revealing—an eye-opener for sure—when those of us who worked together and have remained friends after retirement get together socially.

We try not to just talk fire rescue stuff, but sometimes we can't help it.

Although I have said many times that the ghosts remain, it doesn't mean they control my every thought. I believed in taking good care of myself after coming home from shift. That could mean getting some sleep; eating good, healthy food; and definitely exercising. For some, it meant hugging their children; for me, it certainly meant hugging my fur-children. Sometimes, it means indulging in a huge cheeseburger, fries, and a Coke or maybe a beer, then heading to bed. Or it could mean a great strong cup or two of coffee before a long, sweaty run. Everyone is different, but it's important to find a way to expel the prior shift's imprint.

But, of course, none of us can erase the memories completely, and we find ourselves rehashing them when we're together socially. But we also find ourselves constantly asked to rehash them in public—before retirement when we stopped into a grocery store in uniform on our way home, and after, when a civilian asked us what we did for a living, back in the day. I was told by a retired friend that this is just like picking a scab. That's pretty much right, but it's almost impossible to avoid.

Almost every firefighter-paramedic that I have known has dealt with this scenario. Once you have been identified as a firefighter, the conversation usually goes like this:

"Wow, you're a firefighter! That's great! I'll bet you have seen some things in your career."

I nod at that.

"You get to sleep at the firehouse, right?"

"If we are lucky."

"And you have a pension, right?"

"Yes." I brace myself at this, because I know what's coming next.

"Must be nice to have that and not have to worry about money when you retire."

Must be nice not to risk your life every time you go to work, I think but never say.

"By the way, what's the worst call you have ever run?"

I try to be polite. In my eye's mind, I am thinking about hair, eyeballs, and teeth in a windshield; bodies twisted in unnatural positions from the trauma; fire victims who look like marshmallows left on the fire too long; brains blown out from gunshot wounds; and bodies that succumbed to drug overdoses, diseases, or just old age. I'm thinking about telling people that I am sorry, we did everything we could, but their loved one has died, on and on and on. I'm avoiding thinking about children, even to myself, and I won't tell this person about those calls under any circumstances.

Instead, I say, "Oh, you don't really want to know."

The conversation ends, the other person disappointed to be spared the gory details. But what sticks with me more often than not is the pension comment. I hear it quite often, and other retirees have told me it creates friction with neighbors, strangers, and even family members.

What are we, Unicorns?

It seems to be a common theme. When people saw us in uniform, coming home from a busy twenty-four or forty-eight-hour shift, red-eyed and dragging ass, they were complementary. Some even called us heroes. But now that we are retired, and they see us looking rested, doing normal things, those same people are jealous, frustrated that their taxes pay for our retirement. It costs some of us friendships.

If I just wanted to get rich, if I wanted to live "the easy life," becoming a firefighter-paramedic wasn't going to accomplish that. I started out making $8.55 an hour in 1987, a godsend to me back then. In those early days, I never even thought about a pension. But I do remember an old-time firefighter telling me I would appreciate having one in twenty-five or thirty years.

And I most certainly do.

I say a little prayer of thanks every day, but I also know the majority of men and women who chose this career didn't do it for the money. We took an oath to save lives and protect property.

But it isn't always sideways glances and muttering about the pension. One of the most gratifying aspects of the job is when someone we have saved comes into the firehouse to thank us. Sometimes they write a letter to the chief, who sends it down the chain for us to cherish.

Now, I have to ask: How many people can say there are humans walking around today because of the actions they took on the job?

That, my friends, is priceless.

A MOTHER'S LOVE

Author's note: In honor of my mother, Dorothy, and to give insight on why I reignited my passion for writing, I have to include this composition I wrote many years ago, long before my retirement. She had a tough life. She received only a sixth-grade education, she was disabled, and she was thrown away after thirty-six years of marriage by my father, Arthur. But she told me the only thing she ever wanted to be was a mother. And she was an excellent one.

Approximately 1990: English Composition: Thank you for re-igniting my passion for writing:

From the age of five, I knew that my life would get better.

Looking back now, I find it miraculous not only that I survived but that I have found great happiness and love, despite my background.

I was born in a small town in rural Ohio, to very poor parents who endured a loveless marriage.

We lived in a tiny house without indoor plumbing. My mother kept a pot hidden behind a curtain where we could relieve ourselves in semi-privacy. When our primitive toilet was full, she had the arduous task of carrying it to the outhouse to empty, regardless of the weather.

I clearly remember bath time, which consisted of nothing more than a steel tub filled with water that Mom had heated up on the stove. She is a very talented woman with a heart of gold. She was born poor, lived in poverty her entire life, and is very much a product of her generation. Quite a few women her age who grew up during the depression sacrificed their dreams for those of their husbands and children. She is no exception.

There were plenty of times when all we had for dinner was bread and milk, but I was lucky that my Aunt Nola and Uncle Ralph both worked in my elementary school. He was the janitor, and she was the cook, so she made sure my belly was full whenever I was in school. And Aunt Nola would sneak leftovers out of the cafeteria and bring them over to our house, along with her delicious homemade peanut butter cookies.

Going to school was extremely tough for me, because I never felt good enough. I was not only poor, but I was tall and dark-skinned, too. My American Indian heritage did not serve me well at the time. It seemed to me that all of my classmates were cut from the same blond-haired, blue-eyed cloth. They taunted constantly, calling me "Pocahontas," and they called my older brother, Gary, "Squawman." Jokes on them, though, because even today, at age forty-nine, he embraces that nickname, all six feet, eight inches of him.

Despite my dismal surroundings, I knew that life held many wonderful surprises for me. I recall that my love of books and music became apparent at around age four. Some of my fondest memories of childhood are of my mother listening to the radio and singing or humming along while she ironed clothes. When it was discovered that I was gifted with an ear for music, my parents scraped together twenty-five dollars for an old piano that was on its way to the dump. My mom would turn on the radio, sing along, then ask me if I could play the songs back to her. I proceeded to do just that learning all her favorites: "Hello Dolly," "Red Roses for a Blue Lady," and "Wabash Cannonball," for starters.

I loved to read books, too, and I would devour anything I could get my hands on. Reading stirred my imagination, and it allowed me passage to faraway places where magical things could happen and anything was possible.

My mother always encouraged me to strive for whatever my heart desired. But as time went on, she knew I was restless and nothing good would ever come to me by staying in that small prejudicial town.

When winter hit, my dad would tell us to pack up our belongings, and then we would head south to Florida, where he could find work as a brick mason. We would stay with my older sister, Linda, and her husband, Charlie, until we found a cheap place of our own to live, usually a trailer. This became a yearly ritual when I was almost eleven years old.

Since I adored both my sister and her husband, Florida seemed like the promised land to me. I never felt like an outcast there, because there were so many different nationalities of children, many with darker skin than mine. But like clockwork, my dad would come home at night after a couple of months as spring approached, frustrated and tired, telling us to start packing because we are moving back to Ohio where he could make more money. I was so furious every time they removed me from school just when I had started to make new friends, but that's life when you're a child. I would sob the entire way back to Ohio. I wrote desperate poems and letters to my sister expressing my sorrow, which broke her heart.

Finally, during one of our yearly trips south, my sister and brother-in-law persuaded my parents to let them become my legal guardians. Then I could live with them and go to school. I was only thirteen years old, and my life was forever changed.

I now realize the unselfish love that my mother had for me. In order that I might have a better future, she gave up her youngest daughter.

I am positive that she spent many sleepless nights because of her decision, but it meant that the little Native American girl who never smiled could grow up happy, with a renewed zest for living.

I will be eternally grateful to my mother for her unselfish love.

HEROES OR MERELY OLD WARRIORS, NEW HOUSE, NEW PUPPY, LIVING IN A BUBBLE TO AVOID COVID, REFLECTING, 2021

As I sit here almost six years after my retirement, reflecting on my experiences, reminiscing with colleagues that have remained friends, and congratulating new retirees I had the pleasure of working with, I start to question:

Who are we? Did we matter? Does anyone care about our experiences?

I am reminded of the Bruce Springsteen song, "Glory Days." When those of us who worked calls together get together, we laugh, joke, and congratulate each other on our travels and our health. We indulge in the memories of our primitive living conditions, running calls with little help, saving lives, and feeling good about retiring healthy. (So many of our fellow colleagues never got the chance.) We remember counting the days until we could leave, when we dreamed about sleeping in, taking vacations, and enjoying time with the people who mean the most to us.

I guess old warriors are destined to turn into forgotten heroes, but those of us who lived it will reminisce among ourselves until nobody on the job remembers any of us.

That is life. That is generational change.

I am content knowing that, during my time on the job, we did everything possible to make a positive difference in people's lives. The most gratifying outcome was when someone whose life we saved would come into the firehouse and thank us. That was priceless.

Before the coronavirus pandemic, I was a huge fan of reality TV shows. I said sometimes you just want to enjoy a box of Cracker Jacks and take a break from politics, history lessons, and that exhausting, twenty-four-hour news cycle. Now I cherish time, friends, my home, and my new puppy, Chewie. But most of all, I cherish my personal, special guiding light who has anchored me and loved me unconditionally.

I hope this book inspires, motivates, and entertains you, but most of all, I hope it gives you a glimpse into the trials and tribulations of my life as a female firefighter, a firefighter-paramedic, and a captain. I hope that, once you've glimpsed my improbable journey, you recognize that, whether you dream of being a firefighter or anything else, you understand there's nothing stopping you.

I always say this was the best job in the world, and most of my colleagues agree.

ACKNOWLEDGEMENTS

First, I must thank all of the firefighters and paramedics who worked with me throughout my career, believing in my ability to succeed and ultimately lead. The stories of our time together are the core of This book, and they capture some of the most important and meaningful moments of my life.

A whole crew of people have helped me take some rough stories that I had been developing, based on my reignited passion for writing and lifetime love of reading, and develop them into a complete manuscript and a published book. Thank you, Lari Bishop at Draft Lab, for your expertise and guidance. I am a better writer because of you. You listened to me and believed in my story from the very beginning of this project, and for that I am grateful. Thank-you Alex Head at Draft Lab. Your creative imput and consulting for the interior design was appreciated. Thank you, Sarah Welch, Sara Kocek, and Angela Vanryken at Yellow Bird. Your editorial prowess and professionalism are so appreciated. Thank you, Martha Bullen, for your extraordinary marketing skills and ability to reach many areas that otherwise wouldn't be possible. Thank you, Jeremy Avenarius at Real Avenue Design for creating a beautiful web page. And last but certainly not least, Thank you David Ter-Avanesyan for a beautiful cover and page design.

And I must acknowledge another special person in my life who was instrumental in connecting me to Lari Bishop. James A Keith, my beloved nephew. I fell in love with you the first time I laid eyes on you when you were just a baby. You have grown into an extraordinary man who makes me so proud.

Being a First Responder working and living with others who have the same objective to help those in crisis has been my honor and privilege. I encourage anyone who wants to serve, but especially women who have the desire to enter this noble profession, to go for it. You won't regret it.

ABOUT THE AUTHOR

Cindie Schooner-Ball began her career as a first responder with the fire service in 1987, just a decade after the first career female firefighter in the United States joined the ranks. Over her twenty-eight-year career, she pushed herself to tackle new challenges, earn degrees, and rise into leadership positions. She became an EMT and then a Paramedic, while also earning a degree in fire science.

Cindie recognized early on that to succeed as a woman in a mostly male workplace would require perseverance, grit, and the ability to set boundaries. She learned how to make it clear that she expected respect. When she finally achieved the rank of captain, she was the only woman at that induction ceremony.

Now retired, she loves speaking to people about her experiences as a first responder and as a woman who discovered her passion and ambition in a male dominated industry.

She currently lives with her husband Mark, and her German Shepherd Chewie, in beautiful Florida, the land of palm trees and sand.

* 9 7 9 8 9 8 5 6 8 8 1 0 8 *